# *THE* INTERCESSORS HANDBOOK

*HOW TO PRAY with Boldness, Authority and Supernatural Power*

## JENNIFER EIVAZ

### Chosen

a division of Baker Publishing Group
Minneapolis, Minnesota

Published by Chosen Books
11400 Hampshire Avenue South
Bloomington, Minnesota 55438
www.chosenbooks.com

Chosen Books is a division of
Baker Publishing Group, Grand Rapids, Michigan

Printed in the United States of America

ISBN 978-0-8007-9791-1

Library of Congress Control Number: 2016930717

17  18  19  20  21  22  23        12  11  10  9  8

# Contents

# Foreword

Much like learning a foreign language or reading hieroglyphics, understanding our authority in intercession is a skill that can be acquired through teaching, instruction and practice. Many gifted people find themselves troubled, confused or even plagued by experiences in the spiritual realm because they misinterpret or misapply those experiences, which often leads to fear, anxiety and even depression. Jennifer Eivaz has done a masterful job in her book, *The Intercessors Handbook*, of communicating, in a simple and understandable way, how to access your full authority in prayer in order to take dominion over the earth.

The apostle Paul wrote to the Corinthians and said, "Now concerning spiritual gifts, brethren, I do not want you to be unaware" (1 Corinthians 12:1 NASB). The word *gifts* is not in the Greek text because Paul was not just trying to teach us about spiritual gifts; he was explaining to us how the spirit world works. The Church has lost access to the spirit realm in this postmodern age. We have exchanged the visible for the valuable, and we have washed up on the shores of the logical, tangible and predictable.

*The Intercessors Handbook* is more than a book. It is a step-by-step training manual written to help you comprehend the unseen world. Jennifer hands us the lost keys to the mysteries of the power of prayer and shows us the way to bring the Kingdom of heaven to earth. I highly recommend this book to every believer!

Kris Vallotton, senior associate leader, Bethel Church, Redding, California; co-founder, Bethel School of Supernatural Ministry; author, *The Supernatural Ways of Royalty* and *Spirit Wars*

# Acknowledgments

I want to thank my husband, Ron (www.roneivaz.com), for his endless support and for encouraging me to write this book. He is the love of my life and my very best friend. I am grateful we found each other, and I look forward to many more decades of happiness together.

I also want to thank my Harvest Christian Center family (www.harvestturlock.org) for their amazing support and endless efforts to reach the city and influence the nations. This book was made possible because the HCC family prayed together and experienced God together. Ron and I are proud to pastor such amazing and gifted people.

Steve and Derene Shultz, from the Elijah List (www.elijahlist.com), also deserve special mention for bringing me forward as a featured writer in their publication. Their endorsement resulted in creating the right connections to have this book professionally published. They have also become my trusted friends.

Many thanks to Kris and Kathy Vallotton (www.kvministries.com) for being my pastors and spiritual parents. Their enduring love and faith in me have made me the woman of God that

I am today. They saw good things buried deep inside of my heart, and they pulled very hard to bring those things out. I am forever grateful.

Finally, I want to thank my Lord and Savior, Jesus Christ, for taking me from nothing and fashioning me into who I am today. I was very lost, but now I am found. I was blind, but now I see. Jesus is the reason I do what I do, why I get up in the morning and why I lie down at night. He is everything to me.

# Introduction

Prayer is like breathing. It becomes oxygen to our spirit. When we pray, we feel alive and connected to God. In prayer, we can distinguish His voice and encounter the realm He lives in. Prayer takes the dryness out of our souls and releases refreshing rivers into our world. It is not just something we do for a few minutes here and there. We integrate prayer into our lifestyle and make our lives a living prayer.

I learned to pray in the fires of desperation. It was during those times when I felt my world caving in that I discovered how to reach out to God for answers. With gut-wrenching tears, I would ask Him the tough questions, tell Him all my fears and contend for answers. I rested in knowing God was not offended by my authenticity and would respond just as honestly. I learned how to listen and trust His voice in tough situations. He was working everything for my good. It was all going to be okay.

Many people do not even think about prayer until they are handed a problem they cannot solve. Find out you have a terminal disease, for example, and suddenly you have a prayer life. Get a miracle because of prayer, and now you are committed.

Prayer becomes the first thing you do instead of the last. You have discovered the power of prayer, and you will never be the same.

Intercessors are most often birthed in crisis. Once you have seen the impossible made possible through prayer, something happens on the inside of you. Faith is birthed in your heart, and prayer takes on a fervency in your life. You just know that you know prayer will change what needs to be changed.

Still, we run into situations that seem not to respond to prayer. When this happens, know that God is not withholding His clear promises from you. Rather, there is something you do not understand about His Word or about the spiritual realm. God always has an answer, but we do not always know how to appropriate it. These are the gaps I hope to bridge in this book, helping you connect not only to prayer but also to *answered* prayer.

All the principles of prayer covered in this book are rich treasures excavated through the trials and wildernesses of my life and ministry. I have taught them diligently to my church and to anyone who would listen. Now I am glad to share them with you.

This book was a project held in my heart for several years before the outset of writing it. I did not consider myself a writer and could not find the grace or the time to produce it. Then one day, I received a Facebook message from a prophet and minister living in Anderson, California. Her name was Mary Andersson, and we had known each other for only a few years. Mary receives dreams from God on occasion, and she had been given a dream for me. In her dream, I had written a book about prayer. It was a handbook, she said.

When Mary sent me the dream, I felt the tangible anointing of God come upon me. It felt like a calm liquid, filled with power, on my whole being. From there, I was able to start writing and wrote the first edition of this book, which I self-published.

The first edition was written to my church. We have a unique prayer history, which I will share with you in the chapters of this book, and I wanted something written down that newcomers could read and assimilate. I also knew the book would go farther out, such as to the other places where I minister, but not too much farther.

To my surprise, the book began selling in the United States and even internationally. It sold in Canada, South Africa, Australia, England, Latvia, New Zealand, Japan and a few more places. The content resonated with intercessors. They desperately needed validation and instruction for the things they were encountering in the place of prayer. I was overjoyed to become that bridge, someone who could help them pray with greater confidence in their unique spiritual climates.

Finally, a lovely woman approached me about writing a book for Chosen Books after reading some of my featured articles in the Elijah List. I could not resist the challenge and responded with an enthusiastic yes. We decided to rewrite and expand the handbook, and you hold the result in your hands. I think it is much improved over the first edition, as it is written for a broader audience and includes even more content to help you process the unique work of intercession. My team of intercessors are praying over this book and all those who read it, that prayer would come alive all over the globe and be effective!

# 1

# My Lifeline for Victory

If you were to ask me my maiden name, I would hesitate to say it. That is because I have little identification with my birth name. My biological father abandoned my mother and me when I was a baby. I would express my loss as a young toddler by asking men, even strangers, "Are you my daddy?" My mother offered very few details of her marriage to my father, except to say that he drank too much and had left my home state of Nevada to find work.

He never returned home but made contact again soon after my mother remarried. I was then four years old. He began to pay a small amount of money each month for my care, and Mother allowed him visitation rights once a year. As a young girl, I was excited to see him. Our annual visits, however, became huge disappointments. His behavior could swing from paranoid to jovial to abusive—you never knew what to expect—all fueled by alcoholism and schizophrenia.

This led to a sequence of events that resulted in the book you now hold in your hands, which teaches you how to be an effective and powerful intercessor in and on behalf of the Kingdom of God. I will tell you in this first chapter how I became one such intercessor myself—someone who believes in the spiritual realm that surrounds us at all times and with which we are meant to interact in the authority of Christ—and then, in the remaining chapters, I will give you all the essential tools you need to become an intercessor, too.

What happened next, then, is that my mother, unable to make ends meet as a single parent, moved us back to her home state of California to be near her family. Her sister introduced her to a recently divorced man, a security guard by trade, whom she soon married. He was a faithful member of the Latter-Day Saints (LDS) church,[1] also known as the Mormon church, and we all became LDS members. My new stepfather assumed a father's role in my life, and I was glad to receive the attention.

Mother, on the other hand, had struggled to keep her emotional balance for as long as I could remember. I even had dreams as a preschooler that her head kept falling off. Imagine that! Over time, her frequent episodes of anger, anxiety and depression exhausted me. To cope, I withdrew, doing everything I could to keep my distance. I disengaged from conversation and stayed in my room as much as possible.

As a teenager, I began exhibiting my anger and pain through rebellion. I snuck out of my home at night to attend unchaperoned parties with my friends and boyfriends. I drank heavily, used cocaine and lied about nearly everything because I no longer trusted anyone with my world. I missed several high school classes, writing fictitious notes from my parents to the school office to be excused, and barely graduated.

Between my spiraling rebellion, my mother's emotional issues and some serious financial issues, our family began falling apart. This challenged our connection to the LDS church because we felt unable to meet their high standards. Mormons place an emphasis on good works and strong families, but they lack the empowering of the Holy Spirit to see those things happen. According to their beliefs, those who meet the standard will progress to become a god in the next life. You can imagine our dilemma when we discovered that no matter how hard we tried, we could never be good enough. Discouraged, we stopped attending the LDS church. We had no strength to be in a religion that proved powerless to help us.

As LDS members, we were instructed to reject evangelical Christianity. We thought *we* were the real Christians and the only ones with the truth. I never cared that much for evangelical Christians anyway, my paradigm having stemmed from watching Jim and Tammy Faye Bakker on the PTL television network. I thought they were nuts, and my stepfather and I would watch the show just to mock and make fun of them.

At the same time, I had a few relationships with some Christians who were acquaintances and extended family. As my immediate family began to crumble, I felt inside of myself that some of those acquaintances were praying for me to become one of them. That infuriated me! I responded to that "knowing" by verbally attacking them with whatever I could make up against them—which was a sign I was probably going to turn around soon.

## An Encounter with God

In the midst of all this, my mother's half brother experienced a radical conversion to Christianity. He began serving as a deacon and then later as an elder in a small United Pentecostal church.[2] Their relationship was best characterized as a love-hate relationship with undertones of a long-standing sibling rivalry. I believe this dynamic began when my uncle's father rejected my mother as a stepdaughter when she was very little. No one knows the real reason for it, but he refused to have her live in the home. She went to live with her grandmother as a result, and it drove a perfect wedge into her relationship with my uncle—a wedge that did not stop him from repeatedly inviting us to his church.

Normally, we would not have given his invitations a second thought. But desperation causes you to consider things you would normally pass by. On a Sunday during my first college semester, then, my mother drove my half sister and me to my uncle's church, leaving my uninterested stepfather behind.

It was a culture shock for all of us. As Mormons, we were taught that reverence for God in a church service was demonstrated by a pious and quiet demeanor. This church was completely different. Everything was loud and unrestrained. The people sang extravagantly, and the preachers preached boisterously. It was common for people to clap their hands and shout "Hallelujah!" or "Amen!"

As unreserved as they were in their worship, they were highly reserved in their appearance. They felt women should demonstrate holiness before God by not wearing jewelry or makeup, by growing their hair long and by wearing long dresses. The men kept their hair noticeably short and refrained from growing any facial hair.

On that first Sunday we visited my uncle's church, I sat there and observed as the pastor finished preaching and then took up a guitar and led out in a very moving song. I do not remember his sermon, but I do remember what he sang. He began singing about the nature of Jesus and then sang a question to the congregation. He asked in song, "Are you ready?" When he did, I began to feel something I had never felt before. It felt like liquid warmth poured out on my head and then all over my body, and I was filled with indescribable peace. I knew it could be nothing else but the presence of Jesus Christ. On the inside of me, I understood what was happening and knew I was experiencing Him.

As tears began to fall down my face, a woman sitting next to me asked if I wanted to commit my life to Jesus. Although I had no idea what that meant, it seemed right. With the tears still falling, I nodded my head yes. She led me right then in a prayer to repent of my sins and surrender my life to Jesus Christ.

If that was not enough, the woman then put her hands on me and prayed that I would receive the gift of the Holy Spirit. Although I had no knowledge of the Holy Spirit, something amazing happened. I began speaking in a language I had never learned. This experience is referred to as the baptism in the Holy Spirit and unfolds in Scripture with two primary purposes: the power to witness for Christ and the power to pray.

The first time we see the baptism of the Holy Spirit in history is in Acts 2. There, the Holy Spirit poured out in power on Christ's followers, thus giving them the ability to praise the Lord in the languages of the nations. This got the attention of the visiting internationals and led the way for the message of Christ to be preached to all of them with power. Later, Paul described being empowered by the Holy Spirit to pray in unknown languages, making it possible for him to pray past his own ability and to pray the perfect will of God (see Romans 8:26–27; 1 Corinthians 14:18). Before I knew the purposes for the baptism of the Holy Spirit, I had already begun to move in them spontaneously.

My mother, sister and I came home from that church meeting obviously touched and clearly changed. We had all given our lives to Christ, although I was the only one to be baptized in the Holy Spirit. My stepfather was at home when we arrived and asked me to share what happened. I told him the story and watched tears stream down his face as I shared. That was huge, as I had never seen him cry before.

## A Brush with Intercession

Soon after, the Holy Spirit moved upon me to pray for my stepfather. Again, I did not know this was prompted by the Holy Spirit until I studied it later. It just happened, and I just went with it. While studying for my exams in my bedroom and before I could think about it, I found myself on the floor, calling out to God for the salvation of my stepfather. I was in tears, and I was wailing. I felt like I was giving birth to something.

As the Holy Spirit took the lead, this deep and intense prayer emerged from inside of me. I was not using my own words, nor did the words come from my mind. I was using the Holy Spirit's words, and they seemed to come from deep inside. I could feel power on me strong enough to make my body react. I would compare it to the feeling you have when you touch an electric socket, but not quite as strong.

When the power began to subside, my final words to the Lord were, "Save my stepfather or just let me die." I do not know why I used those words, but not long after, my stepfather saw an announcement for a seminar being held at a local Baptist church. The seminar was going to discuss the differences between Christianity and the Latter-Day Saints. He attended, and through the seminar, he was invited to attend their Sunday church services. He attended right away and made a decision for Christ during the altar call. He also began attending that same church on a regular basis.

I was elated about my stepfather's decision. However, even though my mother and sister began attending church with him, I was not quite ready to do the same. Up to that point, I was content to attend a small charismatic InterVarsity group that met each week on my college campus. At the same time, my uncle was pressing me to attend his United Pentecostal church. Even though I had that amazing encounter with the real Jesus at his church, I knew I needed a church that was a bit more flexible. As a young person, it seemed ridiculous to have to give up cutting my hair and wearing makeup.

Eventually, I did choose my family's new church to be my own, and it was a good short-term experience. It had a very large group devoted to people just my age, which helped me further transition from my old friends to new friends. They also had a class for new believers, where I learned about salvation from the Bible and even began memorizing Scripture. My only issue was that they did not teach about the Holy Spirit, a subject I hungered to know more about.

After about four months, I made a sudden decision, to the angst of my family, to leave the Baptist church and attend the same church as my college InterVarsity leader. It was a Foursquare church that was smaller in size but had more of a connection with the Holy Spirit. My family tried to reason with me that we should all be in church together. I understood their logic, but I hungered for a deeper spiritual experience.

Once at the Foursquare church, I was surprised to see one of my neighbors there. When she saw me, she explained with enthusiasm that she had prayed for my family for years. She also invited me to a small weekly prayer group that met in a house. The prayer group liked to do something they called *spiritual warfare*, and they would go after things they felt the devil was doing in people's lives and in the city. I did not understand all of it, but I liked the spiritual intensity.

I began to grow more interested in prayer and started attending the weekly prayer service at the church. This prayer service was not as intense as the house meeting, but it still helped me feel connected to God. I also liked the feelings that came with prayer, such as joy, peace, power, wisdom and the presence of God.

All of which is to say, my first year as a Christian was wonderful and full of discovery. I was happier than I had ever been in my life. There was peace in my home, and as a family we were growing in our faith in Christ. I was also learning to pray on my own and could feel the presence of God when I did.

I never considered that my faith would soon be challenged by Satan and that prayer would become my lifeline for victory.

## A Reckoning with Evil

When I entered my second year of being a Christian, I was still attending prayer services, but I was becoming more and more troubled. That feeling of peace in my home had vanished, and I did not know why. I was also sensing dark things—a demonic spirit, to be exact—and I had not dealt with anything like that since I had become a Christian. I had, however, experienced it prior to becoming a Christian. In addition to growing up in a false religion, I had connected myself to the demonic realm through some occult practices I did not realize were wrong. I had seen and experienced demonic spirits off and on in my childhood, and this grew in intensity during my teen years. I had never told anyone, and it stopped when I became a Christian. I thought it was all gone, but now it had returned.

One night, at the house prayer service, it all came to a head. As we prayed together, one of the women looked over at me with concern. She explained her concern, saying, "I see a spirit of sorcery standing over you!" The moment she said it, something picked me up out of my chair and slammed me against the wall. I then lost contact with my surroundings as I began to exhibit a strong demonic manifestation. It looked very similar to a grand mal epileptic seizure, with the added bonus of demonic voices coming out of my mouth.

The women, all versed in spiritual warfare and in how to break demonic bondages, were helpless to set me free. Nothing they did or said worked. After three or four hours, the demonic manifestations subsided just enough for my neighbor to feel like she could take me home.

For the next three months, I had terrible nightmares and rarely slept. I could hear piercing screams at night, and my bed and bedroom door would shake on their own. When I walked by windows and doors, I would often hear a loud knocking sound, and sometimes other people noticed it, too.

I prayed to God for freedom night and day. One day, a sense of faith filled my heart, and I spoke boldly to that spirit. It had entered my room again to torment me. I said, "I will never serve you. I will only serve Jesus Christ!" When I said that, the spirit left and never returned. With that, I lost all fear of the demonic and seemed to gain a newfound spiritual authority and genuine spiritual gifts.

Through that experience, I found power in prayer and learned some very valuable lessons. Here are some things I learned:

1. I cannot rely on others to have spiritual authority for me. I have to have it for myself. (See Hebrews 6:1: "Be taken forward to maturity.")

2. I had found my deliverance in prayer and nowhere else because God is bigger than the devil. (See Psalm 18:6, 17: "I cried to my God for help. . . . He rescued me from my powerful enemy.")

3. Prayer is the ultimate display of weakness. God will meet me at my point of weakness and make me strong. (See 2 Corinthians 12:10: "For when I am weak, then I am strong.")

4. We connect to God through prayer. At the same time, prayer is a spiritual weapon against everything that opposes God. (See Mark 9:29 NKJV: "This kind can come out by nothing but prayer and fasting.")

5. We cannot be ignorant about the spiritual realm. We have to learn how to pray effectively. (See Hosea 4:6: "My people are destroyed from lack of knowledge.")

Prayer had become my lifeline, and I prayed more intensely and consistently than ever before. At the same time, I struggled with shame and condemnation in connection to prayer. The spirit realm had opened up to me in unusual dimensions after my deliverance, and my experience was well past the grid of everyone I knew.

Perhaps you can relate to this. Perhaps you have had experiences in prayer that no one around you knows, understands or experiences for themselves. Perhaps you wonder how to process all you have encountered and how to live out God's anointing upon you.

I want you to know there is a way to process it and a way to live out your calling as an intercessor with knowledge, authority and faithfulness. The teachings in this book will equip you for it.

To begin, let's turn to the basics of prayer.

# 2

# The Basics of Prayer

Each of us has the innate instinct to pray, often before we even know God. In crisis and in pain, people often reach past themselves into the invisible realm, hoping to receive favor from a God they hope is there. They are frustrated when they do not receive an answer, because something inside believes and wants to touch God in those moments of desperation.

The instinct to cry out to God emerged soon after the Fall of Adam and Eve. Adam and Eve knew close fellowship with God until sin separated them from His presence. They went from being connected in fellowship to being disconnected, and the pain of separation created a deep cry in all of humanity that followed. Men and women, on their own, began to search for and cry out to God (see Genesis 4:26). God did not ignore their cries but responded with His friendship and fellowship.

But here is the thing. Friendship and fellowship between God and man look as unique as each individual. We see the story of Enoch, for example. The Bible says Enoch walked faithfully with God, and then God took him away (see Genesis 5:21–24). Imagine that! God so delighted in Enoch's fellowship that He superimposed eternity upon him before he ever finished living.

Moses had a different story of fellowship. Moses began having face-to-face dialogues with God. The fellowship and dialogue Moses and God shared became so close that Moses would shine with the glory of God after each of their heavenly conversations (see Exodus 34:29–35).

Or look at the story of Hannah. She was a quiet but tenacious woman who desperately wanted a child. She was barren because God had closed her womb, and her sister-wife, Peninnah, delighted in tormenting her over it (see 1 Samuel 1:6). Hannah was miserable about it, but this did not stop her from petitioning God over and over, year after year. She prayed to God so deeply at the temple one day that the priest watching her thought she was drunk (see verses 12–14). Even then, she continued reaching out to God through Eli, the priest, telling him what she wanted.

Because of Hannah's persistence, God responded to her cry and gave her over and above what she had requested. "You have what you asked for," Eli prophesied (see verse 17). She later gave birth to a powerful son, the prophet Samuel, who became the next judge of Israel.

Hannah had much opportunity to become offended at God and people. Anger often stops people from praying. Instead, Hannah did the opposite and drew near to God, with powerful results.

Prayer is about connection, and we each connect with God uniquely. God is a personal God, and He is also supernatural. For that reason, we may have encounters in prayer that others will not have, and others may not connect to our experiences at times. This becomes part of our unique journey in Jesus and is never meant to bring about feelings of condemnation.

So, how does prayer begin?

## Begin with the Voice of God

The journey of prayer begins with God's voice. God is the Word, and He connects to us through communication.

For example, as I sat in that first service at my uncle's church, I did not just become aware of God's presence. I also became aware of God's voice. It was not an audible voice, but it came to me as a strong awareness with a distinguishable thought. Jesus was saying, *I accept you as you are.* This ministered to me because in the LDS church, I never felt good enough. According to their doctrine, eternity is based on good works. I had failed their standard and felt ashamed as a result. But as Jesus stirred my heart and spoke to me of acceptance, I responded and received Him as my Lord and Savior.

If you are a believer in Christ, you might not have heard His voice in a distinguishable way that you know of. The Bible shows us, however, that no person comes to Jesus unless the Father draws them (see John 6:44). That means if you know Jesus, the Father first spoke to the depths of your spirit to come and receive His Son. You heard God's voice and responded, even if you did not know He was speaking to you.

I watched this happen in the life of one of our church attendees. Stephanie walked into our church one night and sat down at a table. I had never seen her before, and she acted unfamiliar with church culture. At the end of the service, she came over to me, looking confused, and said, "I don't know why I'm here."

Once it was all said and done, Stephanie gave her life to Christ. Our heavenly Father had been speaking to her spirit, even though she did not know it. She followed His voice into our church, not knowing why, and responded to His call of salvation.

## Know That God Still Speaks

God not only spoke to us at salvation, but He continues to speak to us. The writer of Hebrews seems to shout, "Today, if you hear His voice, do not harden your hearts" (Hebrews 3:7–8). That is because God never stops speaking to us. On earth, Jesus spent many hours in prayer, connecting the act of prayer to hearing His Father's voice. He said, "The Son . . . can do only what he sees his Father doing" (John 5:19). When did Jesus see what His Father was doing? He saw it in the place of prayer—and so will we.

I know God still speaks today because I have experienced it. For example, I was in prayer one afternoon in our prayer chapel and heard the word *Asia* in my spirit. That same day, my assistant contacted me, letting me know a woman had been ordering my resources from overseas. That was exciting to me, as this was the first time anyone overseas had shown interest in what I had been teaching. I asked my assistant to connect with her and get her information. We ended up exchanging emails, and it turned out she was a missionary to Central Asia.

"What would it take for you to come and minister here?" she asked.

I responded by saying, "I already heard the word of God for it. Let's set the date, and I'll come!"

Communication is the foundation for all relationships, even with God. He's the Word, which means by His very nature, He is always speaking. Prayer begins by hearing His voice and then trusting He still speaks to us today.

## Respond with Your Own Voice

We have been focused on God's speaking part in prayer. But do you know He is interested in also hearing from you? Mark

Virkler, author of *Dialogue with God*, says that prayer is two-way communication. It is a dialogue, not a monologue. Not only does God speak to you, but also He waits for your voice and responds to it. In fact, E. M. Bounds, that great nineteenth-century theologian who taught much on prayer during his lifetime, wrote, "God has of His own motion placed Himself under the law of prayer, and has obligated Himself to answer the prayers of men."[1]

One of the most powerful and difficult truths to digest is that we have tremendous influence with God. Many people excuse themselves from the exercise of prayer, citing the sovereignty of God in all matters. Others cannot fathom that God would consider our thoughts and opinions because, after all, we lack wisdom and fail often. But God, in His sovereignty, restrains Himself from action until He's heard our voice in prayer. Not only will He respond to our prayers, but also He responds immeasurably more than all we can ask or imagine (see Ephesians 3:20).

For example, the cities of Sodom and Gomorrah fell into terrible sin and depravity. God heard the cries of their victims, and those cries were deafening (see Genesis 18:20 MESSAGE). He was compelled to act. But before He did, He consulted with Abraham. Think of that! God refused to destroy two cities until He consulted with a man on the earth. Abraham then negotiated to develop the criterion by which God could spare those cities: If God could find ten righteous ones, then He would not destroy them. Most of us know the way the story ends—that God did not find the ten and consequently destroyed Sodom and Gomorrah in fire—but let us not lose sight of the incredible moment when God consulted with a man concerning what to do.

Then there is the Syrophoenician woman who found Jesus in the city of Tyre and begged Him to heal her daughter of demon possession (see Mark 7:24–30). Jesus was under clear orders from His Father to minister first to the Jews. Like Abraham, however, the woman demonstrated influence and tremendous faith such that Jesus could not contain His response and released her daughter from the unclean spirit.

Jesus said, "If you remain in me and my words remain in you, ask whatever you wish, and it will be done for you" (John 15:7). Did He say what I thought He said? We can ask whatever we wish? Yes, we can! Answered prayer becomes the rule and not the exception for those who abide in Christ and are immersed in His Word.

Furthermore, we shape our future by what we ask God to do. James instructs us, "You do not have because you do not ask God" (James 4:2). We need to be brave and bring our *big ask* to God so He can respond with a *big yes*.

## Participate in God's Work

As we begin to ask—and ask big—our asking expands beyond our needs and into the needs of others. You see, although God has restricted Himself to our prayers, He continues to watch over people and the affairs of earth, looking for opportunities to show His mercy and goodness.

Take a look at what this passage from Ezekiel says: "I looked for someone among them who would build up the wall and stand before me in the gap on behalf of the land so I would not have to destroy it" (Ezekiel 22:30). Do you know what this means? It means that when God wants to intervene, He will look for a man or a woman who will hear His voice and invite Him, through prayer, to work favorably on behalf of another.

This kind of prayer is called intercession. To *intercede* means "to speak to someone in order to defend or help another person." In this case, we are speaking to God on behalf of someone else, asking Him to help them in some way.

Here is an example. When I was in college and living with my parents, I was driving home late one night when I felt the urge to pray for a young relative. I began to pray in my prayer language with a fierce militancy. The Holy Spirit seemed to take the lead as I made a firm command out loud, not knowing why.

"Get your hands off of her!" I shouted into the air. "In the name of Jesus, I forbid you, Satan, from harming her!"

A week later, my relative and her friend were dropped off at a skating rink by her friend's father. They were about thirteen or fourteen years old. The father, who was not a Christian, went all the way home and then changed his mind, thinking he should go back and check on the girls. When he did, the girls were missing from the skating rink. (Keep in mind this was long before cell phones and text messaging. When someone went missing, you had no way to locate them electronically.) On a hunch, the father waited until the end of the session, only to observe the girls being dropped off at a distance from the facility by two adult males. The girls were then confronted and questioned, but the details of that incident were never communicated. What I do know is that God saw a problem and intervened through an intercessor. Whatever was taking place or was going to take place never happened.

This pattern of intercession began to appear more and more in my life. The Holy Spirit would alert me, usually through a strong impression in my heart, that someone I knew needed prayer. It became normal for this to happen in the middle of the night, too. I also noticed the images of faces—people I knew—appearing in my mind over and over. It took me a while to connect the dots, but eventually I realized it was happening for the purpose of intercession.

Has this been your experience? Have you been prompted in your spirit to pray for others, even waking in the middle of the night with an intense urge to do so? Have you later learned the effect your prayers may have had? If so, you are likely walking in the anointing of an intercessor, and God places great value on your ministry of prayer.

Intercession is a beautiful and powerful extension of Christ's ministry on earth. The Bible says He is our great High Priest who forever lives to intercede for us (see Hebrews 7:25). I take great comfort in knowing Jesus prays for me, both of His own accord and through like-minded men and women on the earth who are called as intercessors.

As an intercessor, I gradually grew in knowledge and skill in handling the spirit realm within the context of intercession. You can grow in this knowledge and skill, too. I often felt, and still do, that the spirit realm was more real than the natural realm, as it affects everything we do. I also developed a keen awareness that, as the Scripture teaches, we are not wrestling with flesh and blood and for that reason must handle everything with prayer (see Ephesians 6:12).

What I did not realize—and what you may not realize, either, for yourself—was that I was being prepared for intercession of a kind that was much greater than I could have imagined. That preparation is part of the process of prayer, too. Let me tell you more about what I mean.

## Let God Prepare You

In college, I participated in the InterVarsity ministry and was asked to be in a leadership role and teach a Bible study. The only problem was that I did not know the Bible. But there was another young man on the team who committed to teaching a campus Bible study. He was really smart, and I would attend his group, take notes and then teach his notes to my group. His name was Ron Eivaz—and we've partnered in the Word and in ministry ever since.

Halfway through our education, Ron and I left California to finish our degrees at Oral Roberts University in Tulsa, Oklahoma. While we were there, the Holy Spirit spoke to both of us. He told us we would return to California and pastor the church we had left behind.

We had attended Bethel Temple in Turlock, California, now Harvest Christian Center, which is a historic Assembly of God church. I had gone to that church for a few years and had decided to never go back. It was legalistic, full of strife and politics, and a turnaround looked impossible. Although I would not resist a clear directive from God, I hoped it would not work out. My husband shared the same sentiment. This was not going to be easy.

Upon our graduation, this church was the only door of ministry open to us. Ron accepted the offered position of associate pastor, and we served as best we could within that context. We were grieved as we watched our pastor fight internal wars left and right. He finally gave up and left to go minister elsewhere. Then, just as the Holy Spirit had said, the church board turned to my husband for leadership, and Ron became the senior pastor at just 27 years old.

We realized soon enough we were not wrestling with flesh and blood, but with diabolical powers that wanted control of the church. Again, I had been prepared well in intercession by that point, but this was a whole new challenge. Over time, the spiritual challenges grew fierce and went beyond the paradigm of anyone I knew. Once more, I was on my own to navigate a unique spiritual climate and figure out how to see spiritual breakthrough in this context through intercession.

## Become a House for the Nations

Knowing that prayer was the key to everything, we began an all-church weekly prayer service. It was sparsely attended at first, but God can do a lot with a little. This prayer service was the needed spark to begin the transformation. Slowly but surely, the church began to shift. Renewal came to the church, the people revived, and the church began to live and bring life to the city and to the nations.

Now, I say that God prepared me for an intercession of a kind much greater than I had ever imagined. What I mean by that is that He took me beyond the personal to the corporate. He brought me to a place of leading our church into great acts of intercession on behalf of our church and then our city—and He may desire the same for you.

We know God cares about these things. How do we know? Because Jesus entered the temple courts one day, eyes blazing with anger, and removed by force the greedy merchandisers misusing the temple for personal gain. "It is written," He said to them, "'My house will be called a house of prayer'" (Matthew 21:13).

We can no doubt sympathize with Jesus going after all those merchandisers, but why did He make prayer the point of it all? It is because nothing happens outside of prayer. Watchman Nee said, "In heaven, God's power is unlimited. But on earth, God's power is manifested to the degree that the church prays."[2] The prophet Isaiah also foretold the assignment of the modern-day Church, saying the Church would become a house of prayer for all nations (see Isaiah 56:7).

God cannot move in cities, let alone nations, outside of the cooperation of His Church. The Body of Christ, which is the Church, must agree with the Head, which is Jesus, before this can take place. Where does the Body come into agreement with the Head and thus become empowered for the assignment? In the place of prayer.

Back at our church, we continued to pray weekly. Then one night, the Holy Spirit invaded the prayer service in a unique way. Ron and I had just returned home from a conference at the International Church of Las Vegas. While there, we had received a special prayer of impartation for greater ministry from the conference speakers.

We came home and attended our prayer service as normal—but that night was far from normal. The atmosphere of the room was electric. You could sense the activity of God, and it charged the atmosphere. During the church services the next day, there was a genuine move of the Holy Spirit for the first time since we began ministering there. People flooded the altars, tears streaming down their faces, all of them wanting more of the power of God. This was the beginning of renewal in our church.

We continued to pray together and watched the church transform proportionately. Over time, we added additional prayer services, noticing the connection between the quantity of prayer and the increase in ministry effectiveness. New salvations, miraculous healings and deliverances, and a growing influence in the city became normal.

A praying church is a powerful church, and prayer keeps a church in the center of God's will. When a church commits itself to prayer, it encounters the supernatural realm in many dimensions. We had learned this through our commitment to pray together in dedicated prayer services each week. Our next journey would be to learn our spiritual authority not only as individuals, but also as a church—and that began with knowing who is in charge.

## Kingdom Prayer Principles

1. Prayer is our lifeline for victory.
2. Every person's journey in prayer is as unique as they are.
3. Prayer begins with the voice of God, and God still speaks.
4. You have influence with God, and He is waiting for your voice.
5. To intercede means to pray and intervene in favor of another.
6. God will prepare you for greater intercession.
7. The Church is a house of prayer for all nations because God restricts Himself to the faith of the Church.

## Thoughts for Reflection

1. Prayer is a journey in relationship with God and deepens over time. How have you seen this to be true in your life?
2. We all have an instinct to pray. How have you experienced this instinct?
3. Are you aware of the voice of God in your life? How has prayer deepened this awareness?
4. How would you describe the difference between personal prayer and intercessory prayer? Do you intercede for others?
5. Have you noticed an increase of spiritual experiences in your life in connection with prayer? Are your experiences positive or negative?
6. It's common to experience a measure of demonic pushback in prayer. Do you feel a sense of victory when it happens?
7. Does your church have life-giving and effective prayer services? If not, could you create a solution?

# 3

# Who's in Charge?

Ron and I were young pastors, but we had a distinct advantage over the previous pastors who had come from the outside. Since we had attended the church as parishioners, we knew the power structures controlling it from within. But incoming senior leaders, one by one, had been left blindsided and defeated, not knowing what they were up against. The pastor before us, for example, tried desperately to navigate the power web, only to end up in the hospital with stress illnesses. For the sake of his physical and emotional health, he had to go minister somewhere else. Elite parishioners, motivated by power and self-interest, were in charge of the church, not the pastors. Pastors wanting to survive our church were either forced to give away their leadership or forced to leave.

Cindy Jacobs, of Generals International, once described how demonic powers stand behind an earthly structure or leader to accomplish their evil intentions. She explained in an article that this was the nature of a "strongman." She then noted how a strongman needs to be overcome by a stronger One, referring to Jesus, and that this is accomplished through the prayers and intercession of the Church.[1] (See Luke 11:21–22.)

In the matter of our church, we discerned quickly that we were dealing with much more than a group of controlling personalities. We were dealing with a strongman—a demonic spirit, to be exact.

How did we make that connection? Two powerful factions in the church had a perplexing habit of placing memorial plaques to deceased relatives in key areas in and around the facilities. We had plaques on walls, shelves, chairs, tables, hymnals and the list goes on. This made the church feel more like a shrine to the dead rather than a life-giving worship center. It also caused a hindrance to making needed facility upgrades. Discussions about remodeling were stalled or rebuffed because that wall or that closet, for example, had been dedicated to someone's memory. The last straw was when one of the factions donated money to build a kitchen inside the church and then named the kitchen after their family name! They were not even dead yet, but the customary plaque was already hanging on the wall, a symbol that sealed their power on that part of the building.

I cannot remember where I read it, but around that time I was looking through a book that described some Scandinavian occult practices from the "old country." It caught my interest, as I am part Scandinavian and it was the dominant ethnicity of our church at that time. What struck me was its reference to ancestral worship and how it had mixed in with Christianity centuries ago in Europe. The description was strangely familiar to our present situation. I knew we were dealing with some type of witchcraft in the church, but I did not have a name for it because it was happening in a Christian context. I brought the information from the book to my husband and a few others so we could pray and strategically act.

Now, Jesus instructed us to bind things in the spirit realm that work against God's Kingdom (see Matthew 16:19; 18:18). To *bind* something means "to tie it up," and we accomplish that by making a specific command with our words (see Mark 11:23–24). Therefore, using our words, we forbade the spirit of ancestral worship from operating in our church, in Jesus' name, and then asked the Lord to send His Holy Spirit to rule and reign instead.

Things did not change overnight, but we persisted in prayer. Eventually, some board members felt impressed by the Holy Spirit to begin removing the plaques from around the church, including the infamous kitchen plaque, until none remained. This process took a few years, but this time there was very little resistance. Each time we removed a plaque, we could feel power being reassigned to its proper place. Power structures were losing their influence, and those involved began exiting the church. The strongman was being dismantled.

These factions had divided this church for an astonishing fifty years before the spirit behind them was broken. The church almost died before things turned around. The pastors before us kept falling into the same trap. They would try to solve the problems relationally without knowing how to deal with them spiritually. They needed to recognize a spiritual strongman was at work and then to show that spirit who was in charge.

## The Demonstrable Power of Prayer

Our situation was not unique. The devil has always gone to church and will continue doing so until Jesus returns. This may be something you are encountering right now in your own church, in fact.

Even Jesus encountered this during His ministry on earth, but He did a much better job of handling it. In the first chapter of Mark, for example, He went to Capernaum with His disciples to teach in the synagogue. While He was teaching, a demon-possessed man openly challenged His authority. Jesus wasted no time casting the spirit out. He then left the synagogue to heal Simon's mother-in-law of a serious fever and followed that miracle with a healing-and-deliverance service that evening. Then, in the dark hours of the early morning, He woke up and prayed before traveling to the nearby villages to do it all again. (See Mark 1:21–39.)

Jesus flowed in the river of power, prayer and spiritual authority everywhere He went. The apostle Peter portrayed Him well, saying, "God anointed Jesus of Nazareth with the Holy Spirit and power, and . . . he went around doing good and healing all who were under the power of the devil, because God was with him" (Acts 10:38). Those possessed with spirits often cried out in His presence as their resident demons challenged His authority. He answered the question of who was in charge by casting them out and setting people free.

## The Root of Power Is Prayer

Here is the important thing to notice. Although fully God, Jesus chose to function as a man anointed of the Holy Spirit on the earth (see Philippians 2:6–8). He was preparing us, through His example, to embrace a new lifestyle anointed by the Spirit of God and fueled by the power of prayer. Jesus demonstrated this lifestyle of prayer and often withdrew to pray alone in the wilderness (see Mark 1:35; Luke 5:16). Prayer was a point of communion with His Father and also the source of His miracle ministry.

For example, one day He infuriated the Jewish leaders by healing a man on the Sabbath. The leaders defined His miraculous healing as work. They argued that work on the Sabbath was unlawful and even worthy of death. Keep in mind that they were not really concerned about the Sabbath but were acting out of jealousy. Jesus told them the secret to His power, saying, "The Son can do nothing by himself; he can do only what he sees his Father doing, because whatever the Father does the Son also does" (John 5:19). Where did Jesus see what His Father was doing? He saw it in the place of prayer.

Another time, the disciples, unable to cast a spirit out of a young boy, brought the boy to Jesus for help. Jesus cast the spirit out of him and then instructed His disciples about it. He said, "This kind can come out by nothing but prayer and fasting" (Mark 9:29 NKJV). Having observed all these things, they took note that Jesus was powerful because He was prayerful.

### The Focus of Prayer Is God's Will

The disciples later asked Jesus, "Lord, teach us to pray" (Luke 11:1). Jesus complied, giving them point-by-point instructions in prayer, also known as the Lord's Prayer, to get them started. As part of His instruction, He taught the disciples to pray for the will of God to be done: "This, then, is how you should pray: 'Our Father in heaven, hallowed be your name, your kingdom come, your will be done, on earth as it is in heaven'" (Matthew 6:9–10).

This teaching for the disciples is also a teaching for us. We, too, need to pray for God's will to be done.

The prophet Elijah demonstrated this concept well. The Lord told Elijah He was going to end a three-year drought in Israel and send rain on the land (see 1 Kings 18). But Elijah did not leave things there. Instead, he climbed to the top of Mount Carmel and postured himself in prayer (see verse 42). Even though Elijah knew what God wanted, he still prayed for it to happen. As he anticipated, it soon began to rain, and God's will was being done on earth as it was in heaven.

God's will being done on the earth requires a person to know the will of God and then to pray it through to completion. Too many people stumble over this concept. Why do we need to pray for something God already wants? It does not seem logical. If God desires something, can't He just make it happen?

The answer is no.

God's will is for everyone to know Him and escape hell, but not everyone does. God's desire is for all children to grow up in safe and nurturing environments, but many do not. God's plan for peace and prosperity on the earth is clear, but much of the earth has missed this blessing. His will is not being done on a lot of levels. Why?

Because we are in charge.

## The Fluctuating History of Power

God gave mankind full authority over the earth back in Genesis, when He created man and woman in His image. Men and women were not intended to function autonomously, but rather in partnership with God as they lived out their assignment. I think this verse explains it well: "The highest heavens belong to the LORD, but the earth he has given to mankind" (Psalm 115:16).

God blessed Adam and Eve when He told them, "Be fruitful and multiply; fill the earth and subdue it; have dominion" (Genesis 1:28 NKJV). Apparently, God gave Adam and Eve so much authority over the earth that they had the power to lose it. They did not know they were giving it up, but they had the free will to be flippant with their authority, even to the point of giving it to someone else. Through deception and disobedience to the command of God, Adam and Eve did just that. They gave their authority away to Satan, and Satan ruled the earth for several thousands of years.

That is, until he met Jesus.

Three times, Jesus referred to Satan as "the prince of this world" (see John 12:31; 14:30; 16:11). During one interaction between Jesus and Satan, we see the devil attempt to broker back the authority given to him by Adam in exchange for Christ's allegiance and worship.

In that encounter, Jesus had been fasting for forty days in the wilderness. The Holy Spirit led Him to do this in preparation for His upcoming ministry. Then, in His weakened state, He was tempted by Satan, who was trying to gain the advantage.

We read in Luke 4 that the devil took Jesus to a high mountain and showcased all the glory of his earthly kingdoms. Then he made a very grandiose offer, saying, "All this I will give You, if you will bow down and worship me" (see verses 6–7). Jesus did not negotiate that day but instead took the earth's dominion back from Satan by paying man's penalty for sin on the cross. Only a perfect Man could pay this penalty in order to strip Satan of his authority and restore that authority to mankind, as our heavenly Father originally intended.

Jesus died and is now alive, and He has taken Satan's keys (see Revelation 1:18). Keys are a symbol of authority, so if Satan has no keys, that means he has no authority. Just think about that! When we encounter demonic resistance, then, we do not take no for an answer. In Christ, we hold the keys of authority He gained for us. Because of Christ's sacrifice and resurrection, we are once again in full charge of the earth, and we are endowed with all of the spiritual resources we need to steward it.

Our assignment is clear: to bring forth God's will on earth as it is in heaven. This depends first on our prayers and intercession.

It depends next on our stewardship and actions. It is now our privilege to press into a God-ordained authority shift on the earth that favors the Kingdom of God (see Isaiah 9:7).

By His own design, God does not override our will and authority in the earth's sphere. We have been charged with inviting the will of God into the earth, and when we fail to do so, God's will does not happen. Many Christians, unaware of this truth, give their spiritual authority away on many levels. When resisted or demonically attacked, they remain prayerless and passive, not recognizing the spiritual dimension behind what is happening. And much of what is happening behind the scenes is spiritual.

Just before His ascension, Jesus told His disciples, "All authority in heaven and on earth has been given to me. Therefore go" (Matthew 28:18–19). He charged the disciples—and us—to go. But when we go, we need to know we will encounter resistance. This is why we need to know our spiritual authority.

Let's turn to a deeper exploration of that subject now.

## Kingdom Prayer Principles

1. Our spiritual authority rests in knowing who's in charge.
2. Jesus connected His ministry of power to His lifestyle of prayer. He said, "I only do what I see the Father doing."
3. Demonic powers, or the "strongman," can stand behind earthly structures or leaders to accomplish their evil intentions. We will not be able to solve problems relationally that are actually problems spiritually.
4. When we "bind" things in the spirit realm that work against God's Kingdom, we are actually "tying it up." We do this by using our words and commanding it to be done.

5. In Christ, we hold the keys to spiritual authority. We are now pressing into a God-ordained authority shift on the earth that favors the Kingdom of God.

## Thoughts for Reflection

1. Is there any area of your life in which you've given your authority away? Are you ready to take it back?
2. Have you considered that a person opposed to the Holy Spirit could be the agent of a strongman? How would you know for sure?
3. Many Christians try to change a person who is the agent of a strongman through relationship and fail at it. Since it is a spiritual issue, how, then, should you handle this kind of problem?
4. Jesus prepared us, through His example, to embrace a lifestyle anointed by the Spirit of God and fueled by the power of prayer. How are you experiencing this truth?
5. Have you experienced jealousy or criticism from others for your prayerfulness, your answered prayers or your ministry? Does that hinder you or make you self-conscious in some way?
6. Have you considered that God's will is not done without the prayers and cooperation of His Church? How does this motivate you?
7. How do you know for sure that you are praying in line with God's will?

# 4

# Our Spiritual Authority

In Luke 10, Jesus sent His seventy disciples out ahead of Him, two by two, to prepare the various cities for His ministry. He readied them with an uncomfortable truth, saying, "Go! I am sending you out like lambs among wolves" (verse 3). It was a warning about what they could expect from the people they would meet and an instruction to stay calm, no matter what.

We can presume that when the disciples entered the city territories, the resident spirits challenged their authority, because they were later excited to report back to Jesus how the spirits submitted to them in His name. Jesus then further clarified their spiritual authority, saying, "I have given you authority to trample on snakes and scorpions and to overcome all the power of the enemy; nothing will harm you" (verse 19). This marked the beginning of a true authority shift on earth toward the Kingdom of God—an authority shift we, too, get to live out.

It is an authority shift the prophets Daniel and Isaiah had long ago foretold. In Daniel's words, "Then the sovereignty, power and greatness of all the kingdoms under heaven will be handed over to the holy people of the Most High. His kingdom will be an everlasting kingdom, and all rulers will worship and obey him" (Daniel 7:27). And according to Isaiah, "Of the greatness of his government and peace there will be no end. He will reign on David's throne and over his kingdom, establishing it and upholding it with justice and righteousness from that time on and forever" (Isaiah 9:7).

Spiritual authority was delegated first to the disciples and then to every believer in Christ. We have all authority in His name and the capacity to subdue anything that hinders His Kingdom from expanding. And while this is a powerful truth, it is something we need to learn how to live.

## We Are Meant to Overcome

In the first chapter, I shared about my deliverance from occult spirits during a house prayer meeting. There is actually a bit more to that story that connects to what we are discussing here about learning our spiritual authority.

Right before I entered that contention, I encountered the voice of God in an unusual way. I was in bed late one night, listening to a Christian radio station, and had the volume turned low so it would not keep me awake. Before I fell into a deep sleep, the volume turned up high on its own. The radio voice seemed to shout one phrase: "You have to understand your spiritual authority!" Then the volume went down again. I had not touched the volume dial at all.

As a new Christian, I was experienced enough in the paranormal not to react to what had just happened. I knew it was supernatural, but I was not afraid of it. At the same time, I was too inexperienced to see what God was trying to do. He was warning me of things to come and instructing me, all in one moment, and that warning and instruction was this: I was not going to be able to avoid a battle with demonic spirits coming my way. Instead, I needed to overcome them—and I did, once I understood my spiritual authority.

You see, we are meant to overcome those spirits. We have been given all authority and empowerment by the Holy Spirit to do so.

This is something my church has learned to live out, as well. One example has to do with the spiritual leadership we knew the children in our city needed.

For years, my husband had led our church to reach out to the city school system by meeting the material needs of kids. We had provided clothes, shoes, socks, coats, underwear, backpacks— you name it, we gave it, and kids were getting much-needed help. We even brought in quality ministry teams to do anti-bullying and anti-drug assemblies in our schools and continued those messages at special church functions to which we invited all the kids to come.

We were faithful to meet the physical needs of those kids, but they still needed spiritual instruction. Very few parents took their kids to church on Sundays, and kids without God are always kids without hope. We had to do something!

My husband spoke to the school district about renting a room each week to offer a voluntary Kids Club to the students. Kids Club would offer instruction about Jesus and the Bible and impart important life skills in a fun-filled environment. We knew parents would send their kids to it because it would be free and alleviate their need for childcare in the afternoon.

But the idea turned into a wrestling match with the district. They would approve it one day, only to reject it the next. Back and forth it went until the idea was finally stalled. It looked like it would be tossed out.

At the same time, our children's pastor was learning to see these things as spiritual problems and not to take no for an answer. I had encouraged her to get more aggressive in prayer about the situation. She finally did something about it during an all-night prayer service. She took a designated prayer team to the targeted school site and then to the district office to intercede. Three more prayer teams did likewise during the night and early-morning prayer shifts. We remembered Jesus' instruction to pray for God's Kingdom to come and for His will to be done. We also used our words and commanded the demonic spirit resisting the Gospel to be bound in Jesus' name. As we interceded, we felt a sense of faith that circumstances would shift in our favor.

The very next week, we received the good news: Kids Club had been approved by the district. We assembled ministry teams, wrote lesson plans, distributed flyers and headed onto the campus. Within a few weeks of ministry, one hundred students were in attendance, which signaled us to plan for more schools. This ministry was going to be effective!

What we were doing was continuing an ongoing authority shift in our city for the Kingdom of God. This authority shift began centuries ago, with Jesus and His disciples. Jesus gave His disciples spiritual authority to overcome any spirit that attempted to hinder their message about the Kingdom. It is clear that being a follower of Christ does not mean avoiding demonic resistance, but rather learning to overcome it.

## We Have Been Given Authority

Understanding our spiritual authority has been a progressive revelation in my life. I do not know everything there is to know, but I have learned some key truths that will help you grow in your authority and pray more effectively. Let's take a look at each one.

## Authority Where We Have Overcome

One Christmas Eve, we received a phone call on our church emergency line. A man was having problems with his stepson. My husband had ministered during the previous Sunday's church service about the need for fathers to pray with their families, and this father had decided to pray for his family for the first time at their Christmas Eve dinner. He did not know, however, that his stepson had been participating in occult activities. As the father prayed a simple prayer over the meal, the stepson began to levitate off the ground. This shocked the family, of course, and they did not know what to do, so they called the church.

A small group of us went out to help. We arrived at their home and talked briefly with the young man. He now stood firmly on the ground, no longer levitating. However, you could feel the demonic presence inside of him.

The team began to pray for his deliverance but could not get him free. Then it was my turn to pray. I took hold of the young man by the shoulders and commanded the spirit to go. The young man began to exhibit unnatural tension in his body. That was my signal that the spirit was losing power and about to break. Within thirty seconds or less, it left. The young man came to himself, gave his life to Christ and began attending our youth group.

Why could I authorize freedom when the others could not? Because we walk in spiritual authority in the areas we have personally overcome. As Revelation 2:26 says, "To the one who is victorious and does my will to the end, I will give authority over the nations." I had experience with the occult in my past and had overcome it. Therefore, I could walk in greater authority to pray against it.

Again, the Christian life is all about overcoming. Overcoming implies gaining mastery over something, be it poverty, depression, bad relationships, perverse tendencies, drug addiction or something else. These problems were issued to each of us, one way or another, by the demonic kingdom. The Lord said once to Cain, "Sin is crouching at the door, eager to control you. But you must subdue it and be its master" (Genesis 4:7 NLT).

Although the battle looks different from person to person, it is a battle that must be fought. We first overcome these personal issues and any spirits attached to them, and then we have the faith to authorize freedom while praying for and ministering to others. It works that simply and is extremely rewarding to know how to lead others out of the hell-grip you were once in yourself.

### Authority for Tasks Assigned to Us

Another way spiritual authority works is that God gives a territorial mandate to a person—such as a city, nation or people group—and the Holy Spirit authorizes that person for the task. For example, during a prayer service detailed in the book of Acts, the Holy Spirit spoke, saying, "Set apart for me Barnabas and Saul for the work to which I have called them" (Acts 13:2). Also, we see in the Scriptures that the apostles Peter and Paul received distinguishing spiritual authority to evangelize two people groups. Paul was assigned to the Gentiles, while Peter was assigned to the Jews (see Galatians 2:8). Even today, God assigns men and women to evangelize different regions and nations. Consider Reinhard Bonnke's call to evangelize Africa, Dr. Heidi Baker's call to serve the people of Mozambique and Mother Teresa's enduring work in Calcutta. The examples abound.

When such assignments are given, the spirit realm recognizes a person's authority in that place. The angels align to assist the authorized person as they carry out their assignment, and the demonic realm recognizes that person as having specific authorization and reacts accordingly, as well. As we read the stories of Peter and Paul in the book of Acts, for instance, we see Peter was let out of jail at least twice by angels (see Acts 5:19; 12:7) and that Paul was, too (see Acts 16:26). The demons also knew Paul by name, recognizing his spiritual authority above the authority of other people (see Acts 19:15). We see Paul and Peter were also men of worship and intense prayer, which must have been the fuel that helped them accomplish the assignments they were authorized to do.

### Authority to Ask for More

Another way to receive spiritual authority is to ask God for it. For example, David was the promised king of Israel, but we see him receive his authority in stages. He first led military armies, then Judah and finally Israel. Not everyone is called to lead an entire nation, but we all are promised an inheritance in the nations. Psalm 2 teaches, "Ask me, and I will make the nations your inheritance" (verse 8). With that in mind, recognize that spiritual authority can grow and that asking God to give you spiritual authority is a prayer He encourages and will answer.

My experience in praying for more spiritual authority is that it is not usually given in an instant but is given over time as we seek Him. You see, prayer is a form of humility. When we humble ourselves, God will lift us up (see James 4:10). Our humility opens divine pathways for elevation, and spiritual authority comes in the form of opportunities. Stewarding those opportunities then results in a further increase of opportunities.

We know from the Word that each of us is given a measure, or distribution, of faith and a sphere of authority. Romans 12:3 says, "Do not think of yourself more highly than you ought, but rather think of yourself with sober judgment, in accordance with the faith God has distributed to each of you." And 2 Corinthians 10:13 says, "We, however, will not boast beyond proper limits, but will confine our boasting to the sphere of service God himself has assigned to us, a sphere that also includes you." In both these verses, the same Greek word is used to describe our apportioned faith and authority. It is the word *metron,* which suggests that we are anointed to minister within a God-assigned boundary. When we function within our *metron*, we see our spiritual authority produce something.

We see another principle in the Word about stewardship. As the Parable of the Talents teaches, when we steward what we have, God increases it (see Matthew 25:14–30). In other words, your sphere (*metron*) will grow as you are faithful with what is presented to you. God rewards the faithful with more. This is a clear principle demonstrated throughout the Bible.

### Authority When Serving Spiritual Leaders

In the Bible, we see that individuals like Moses, David and the apostles Paul and John were people with great spiritual authority—and certain people do carry a great amount. You might not have that level of spiritual authority on your own, but when you partner from the heart with others who do, you can walk in their authority as you help them carry out their God-given mandate.

For example, in Numbers 11, we see Moses complaining to God about the burden of leading God's people (see verses 11–15). In response, God devised a plan. He told Moses to gather seventy elders at the tent of meeting. As they came together,

God took of His Spirit already upon Moses and transferred it to those elders. This anointing, once conferred, made it possible for the elders to help Moses lead the people just like Moses would. Strangely, two men who were listed among the seventy did not make it to the meeting place but stayed in the camp. When the Holy Spirit came upon the 68 elders at the meeting, the two missing elders also began to prophesy in the camp, signifying the Spirit upon Moses had come upon them also. This did not mean these men were prophets. Rather, it was a sign that the Spirit was on them and that they were authorized to lead alongside Moses.

We see a similar pattern with the apostle Paul and his spiritual son, Timothy, whom he addresses as "my true son in the faith" (1 Timothy 1:2). We are introduced to Timothy in Acts 16, at the start of Paul's second missionary journey, when Paul picks up the young disciple in Lystra. Timothy assists Paul, shadowing his ministry, and learns to assimilate Paul's ministry values. Paul later writes to Timothy, "You . . . know what I teach, and how I live, and what my purpose in life is. You know my faith, my patience, my love, and my endurance" (2 Timothy 3:10–11 NLT). Finally, we see a measure of Paul's anointing and authority being given to Timothy through the laying on of Paul's hands (see 2 Timothy 1:6). This spiritual act is patterned after the Old Testament patriarchs, who passed their spiritual blessings on to their sons through the laying on of hands, an act given the full backing of heaven.

I have seen this principle at work in my own ministry. I walk in the office of a prophet, as described in Ephesians 4:11, having been recognized by my church and other ministries in this spiritual gift. Now, there are different kinds of prophets. Some prophets see the word of the Lord in visions, trances and dreams and are often referred to as "seers." Other prophets perceive or hear the word of the Lord through impressions, the inner voice or an audible voice. These distinctions have their roots in the Old Testament, and we still see them at work today.

I am a seer prophet and lead a company of intercessors and prophetically gifted people who see the voice of God much as I do. The anointing on me in my *metron* has likely come upon them and is expressed in a similar way. If I were a different kind of prophet, or if this same group of people were aligned with a prophet in a different *metron*, the way most of them receive the prophetic word would probably be different. The anointing flows down from leaders to those who serve with them to enable them to run together.

## We Are Invited to Exercise It

Once we know our spiritual authority and the ways in which it is distributed to us, we need to exercise it. We are being invited to discover our God-given spiritual authority so that we can be effective in bringing God's will to earth. So, how do we become effective?

Spiritual authority is first revealed in prayer, and then we learn through trial and error how to step into it. This means we will not walk in its fullness all the time, especially at the beginning.

I know this from experience.

In one particular instance, a friend from college called me up and told me her husband was in the hospital. I immediately went to see him and began praying for his recovery. He had been declared brain-dead after reacting to medication given to him by hospital staff. Over the next few weeks, I spent much time in prayer for his recovery and visited him every day, sometimes at midnight and one a.m. Despite much effort in prayer to revive him, he passed away, leaving behind his wife and four children.

Afterward, I was shocked at a visiting pastor's comments. "This is God's mercy," he said. *How could that have been God's mercy*, I thought, *when a father dies and leaves his wife and four young children behind?* As a mother of two young children myself, I simply could not accept his statement. At the same time, I knew that my prayers for the man had not been effective.

In contrast, look at what happened when the apostle Peter encountered a similar need for prayer. While traveling through Joppa, he learned of the death of a beloved disciple named Tabitha (see Acts 9:36–41). The first thing he did was kneel next to her body and pray. We do not hear the details of that prayer or what God spoke to Peter's heart, but we do see the results. Peter called her back to life, and she responded to his authority by opening her eyes.

How did Peter authorize resurrection power in the life of that disciple? If I knew that secret, I would have raised the dead by now, including my neighbor! I have come to recognize the Bible is full of legislation, namely spiritual laws that govern our heaven-to-earth connection, and we must grow in our knowledge and power to exercise them. Unanswered prayers are the result of not knowing or understanding spiritual laws that are tucked away in the Word of God and revealed to us in the place of prayer. As James taught, "The prayer of a righteous person is powerful and effective" (James 5:16).

Do you want to be effective in prayer? Here are a few spiritual laws to consider.

## Pray the Will of God

Many people do not pray effective prayers because they do not understand what the will of God really is. Things authored by Satan are often credited to God out of ignorance. We need to remember what Jesus said: "The thief comes only to steal and kill and destroy; I have come that they may have life, and have it to the full" (John 10:10). This offers us a helpful rule of thumb: If something is stealing from you, killing you or destroying you, then the source is Satan and not God. God's will for us is full and abundant life, and our prayers need to reflect these differences.

### Pray in Faith

Once you know the will of God and you have asked God for it, do not start reasoning as to why it will not happen. Remember what else Jesus said: "Therefore I tell you, whatever you ask for in prayer, believe that you have received it, and it will be yours" (Mark 11:24). We are to believe that God has answered our prayers *before* we see it happen, not after.

How do you know if you have faith? By what comes out of your mouth. Again, Jesus said, "Truly I tell you, if anyone says to this mountain, 'Go, throw yourself into the sea,' and does not doubt in their heart but believes that what they say will happen, it will be done for them" (verse 23).

Let me share a personal example to help you understand what I mean. Our son was diagnosed with a neurological disorder at age four that affected his ability to speak and comprehend language. At the time of diagnosis, he could not even say his name. My husband and I did much prayer and fasting about it. We also put him in therapy five days a week, which continued for seven years, although it lessened in quantity over time.

At the onset, Ron and I made a firm decision in prayer about our son's healing. The Bible says that healing belongs to us in Christ (see Isaiah 53:5 and 1 Peter 2:24). Our prayer went something like this: "We thank You, Jesus, that because of the cross, our son is healed." This is how we prayed and positioned the situation personally and before others. That does not mean we never discussed his symptoms or his diagnosis with medical staff, friends, family or school personnel along the way. We did. In prayer, however, we never changed our words, even in the tough seasons, when healing appeared out of reach. Our words remained the same because our faith remained the same: "Our son is healed in Jesus' name!"

I am thrilled to share that our son is now healed, fluent in speech and comprehension, fully mainstreamed in his junior high school and no longer in need of special education or resource support. This was a God-given miracle, given the severity of his condition, and a testimony of Jesus to our church, his therapist and the school system. It is an example of what praying in faith can look like.

If you have positioned your faith on a clear promise from God, then take note of your words. If you are wavering in what you believe, you will become incongruent in prayer. This breaks the heaven-to-earth connection, causing your prayers to go unanswered.

### Pray in Agreement

Lastly, let's look at another word Jesus gave about how to pray. He said, "Truly, I tell you that if two of you on earth agree about anything they ask for, it will be done for them by my Father in heaven" (Matthew 18:19). The Greek word for *agree* in this passage is *symphōneō*, which sounds a lot like our English word for *symphony*. It means "to harmonize and sound together." This means that when we come together in prayer over the will of God, we need to be praying the same thing. When we do that, it becomes a sound irresistible to our heavenly Father, and He responds to that sound favorably.

Going back to the story of my friend from college, I learned after her husband died that his treatment was not in agreement with our prayers. After he died, I asked the Lord to tell me what happened. He said, "Ask about the opiates." I researched it and learned my friend's husband was being given the strongest dose of sedation, at the permission of his family, since he was not expected to live. This is a common protocol for brain-dead patients. It keeps their body from tremors and convulsing but hastens their death at the same time.

In other words, we were praying for him to live while he was being prepared to die. We were not in agreement, and our prayers did not get answered. This all happened in ignorance, of course, and if I had known the difference existed, I would have communicated with his family about it from the beginning. That is a tough situation to address, but to pray effectively, we have to understand and align with spiritual laws.

Intercessors are often found standing—more like battling— between a problem and a promise from God. They are the freedom agents who legislate the spiritual laws in the land and have to know, without a doubt, their authority in Christ. The force of faith and the gumption to command every spirit to fall in line is what brings forth real and tangible victory into cities and nations.

Know this: Behind every revival in history was an intercessor. Behind every nation that opened its doors to the Gospel was an intercessor. Intercessors can shape history from their prayer closet, causing the impossible to be made possible.

Does that inspire you? Are you ready to be the man or woman who says yes to the assignment of prayer? If so, get ready for the adventure of a lifetime. It is time to claim the territory of God's Kingdom.

## Kingdom Prayer Principles

1. We are being invited to discover our God-given spiritual authority so we can be effective.

2. Spiritual authority can grow. Asking God for more spiritual authority is a prayer He encourages and will answer.

3. Many people do not pray effective prayers because they do not know what the will of God really is. Things authored by Satan are often credited to God out of ignorance.

4. Prayer goes unanswered when we violate spiritual laws that govern our heaven-to-earth connection.

5. Intercessors are often found standing—more like battling—between a problem and a promise from God.

## Thoughts for Reflection

1. We have spiritual authority in the areas we have personally overcome. What are those areas in your life? How has your personal authority in those areas helped someone else?

2. Why is faith necessary for answered prayer? How do you know whether you are operating in faith or not?

3. Do you pray with a prayer partner or with a prayer group? Are you conscious of being in agreement as you pray? How have you seen the results of this type of prayer?

4. Has God spoken to you about a specific assignment for ministry? How are you seeing spiritual authority and aptitude in that area?

5. Are you aligned and serving someone who has more spiritual authority than you do? In what ways have you recognized more effectiveness in your life because of that relationship?

6. Are there any losses in your life or in the lives of people you know that you have credited to God when you should have credited them to Satan?

7. How confident are you that your bold prayers are being heard and will be answered by God?

# 5

# Are Territorial Spirits Real?

As new pastors, my husband and I had to learn how to lead a difficult church. I have already mentioned that our church contained an assortment of power structures, all vying for dominance. Also spread within those structures was an enmeshment of long-standing families, mostly third generation, who were in leadership roles and yet did not demonstrate any evidence of salvation. The feel of church services at the beginning of our time there reminded me of what services were like at the Latter-Day Saints church I had attended—highly religious and lifeless. I knew that if God had called us to this church, then He would have to show us how to lead it.

Now, a church is not the same as a business organization. You cannot solve church problems by relying on rational ideas, logical formulas or systems used in the secular realm. Church issues are spiritual issues at their core and have to be addressed spiritually. The church is first a spiritual organism. Jesus underscores this thought by explaining to Peter that His Church—the universal

Church—is built on the rock of the Word, referring to Himself, and that the gates of hell will not overcome it (see Matthew 16:18).

With that in mind, we attacked each issue in prayer and waited on the voice of Jesus—His specific instructions to our hearts—which then became our secret battle plans to turn each situation around.

One afternoon, the Holy Spirit spoke to my husband to change the name of the church from Bethel Temple to Harvest Christian Center. The church, eighty years old at the time, had held the name Bethel Temple for at least fifty of those years. The name carried a lot of history and sentimentality. It also carried a negative reputation, because some congregants had troubled the city over the decades through politics and shady business dealings. With this in mind, Ron felt he could convince the church board of the need for a new beginning.

"We need to fix our reputation in the community, and we need to prophesy to our future," he explained.

It seemed simple enough.

What we did not know, however, was that the Holy Spirit had just engaged a territorial spirit.

During the special business meeting that was called to vote on the new name, we watched our dissenters finesse and manipulate the crowd to oppose the change. The ballots were cast and then quickly tallied. We were crushed to learn the membership had denied the declaration of a new name by only three votes. It was a discouraging blow, and neither Ron nor I slept that night.

Ron met with some church leaders the next morning to discuss the outcome and to strategize the next steps. He and two boardmembers heard the same prophetic instruction.

"Run it again in ninety days," the Holy Spirit said.

They decided to put the name change before the church one more time—a gutsy maneuver by all previous standards.

Ron kept a great disposition before the church during this time, acting as if nothing had gone wrong. Behind the scenes, we prayed persistently for the will of God to come to pass.

A few months later, Ron spoke to the church on a Sunday to reintroduce the name change. This time, he stepped into his authority, outlining the situation more clearly.

"God has spoken to my heart about changing the name for several good reasons," he said, "mainly that it's time for a fresh start and a fresh focus. We are going to vote on this a second time, and I prayerfully ask that you would receive my leadership about this issue."

Things really shook throughout the church at that point. It was politics and strife, as usual, and a heavy spiritual oppression filled the air.

The night before the vote, I had an intense dream. In the dream, a spirit in the form of an Asian woman appeared to me in my bathroom mirror. She stared at me, her eyes full of hate, and then she began to torment and threaten me.

I am not sure why the spirit was Asian, but in dream language, a mirror is often a symbol for identity. This made sense to me, since we were fighting for our identity as a church. The dream uncovered the truth: We were not just having strong differences of opinion over the name change. We were in a spiritual fight, and this spiritual fight was playing itself out in the natural realm.

The spiritual intensity of the dream is still hard to describe, as it was like nothing I had experienced before. But when I woke up, thanks to the dream, I knew in my spirit that the vote was ours. This territorial spirit, assigned to impair our identity, had finally been overpowered. I knew this happened as a result of our continued prayers.

As I expected, the vote that next evening was much in favor of the name change, and we have been Harvest Christian Center ever since. Over time, our reputation in the community has grown and a new identity has emerged, just as Ron foretold.

I have experienced this truth over and over. When God gives a directive to advance on something and it is met with opposition, we can assume there is some type of territorial spirit behind it. We have to consider the spirit of the matter and recognize that we do not live just in a natural world.

## We Live in Two Realms

As Christians, we are privileged to have dual citizenship. We are citizens of earth and citizens of heaven at the same time (see Philippians 3:20). Many believe we receive our heavenly citizenship only after we die. The Bible, however, illustrates how connected to heaven we are while living on earth.

For example, when we pray on earth, our spirit manifests in heaven before the throne of God. The book of Hebrews gives this description: "Let us then approach God's throne of grace with confidence" (Hebrews 4:16). We often read verses like this with a rational mind, reducing them to metaphors. But many times they are true descriptions of what is happening in the heavenly places as we engage the Lord in prayer on earth.

How is it that we can approach the throne of God in heaven while we are here on earth? It happens in the place of prayer, the place where heaven and earth unite.

Another example is illustrated in a prayer made by King David. He says to the Lord, "May my prayer be set before you like incense" (Psalm 141:2). On the surface, this appears to be an intimate prayer that uses a poetic picture to express David's heart. This is more than a beautiful prayer, however. King David here reveals what happens in heaven as we pray on the earth. Remember the glimpse of heaven given to us in the book of

Revelation, including the throne room of God? One throne room scene depicts four living creatures and 24 elders, each with a harp and a golden bowl of incense, and these "golden bowls full of incense . . . are the prayers of God's people" (Revelation 5:8).

I find it comforting that my prayers transcend earth's realm and become fragrant incense before the throne of God. Do you? It goes to show we are living in two realms at the same time, a natural one and a spiritual one.

Being citizens of heaven puts us into direct spiritual conflict on the earth, however. King Jesus leads a kingdom invasion through us, displacing what used to belong to Satan. These conflicts appear in many different forms and dimensions, and if we are not aware, we will fail to connect that they are rooted in the spiritual realm.

Consider how often Jesus and His disciples cast out demonic spirits from people as they ministered on earth. How often do *we* set people free of spirits in our modern society? In our Western society, it is not nearly as frequent. Is it possible we classify too many spiritual problems as emotional or medical problems because we do not discern where they come from? Do we resort to ineffective natural solutions for life's problems that can be solved only in the spirit realm? The apostle Paul warned us against this, saying, "For our struggle is not against flesh and blood, but against the rulers, against the authorities, against the powers of this dark world and against the spiritual forces of evil in the heavenly realms" (Ephesians 6:12).

Because we live in two realms, it is normal for us to encounter the spiritual realm in the context of prayer. Prayer reaches into the unseen, to the very throne room of God, to procure miracles for impossible situations. But there are sinister territorial spirits, malevolent to the core, that stand behind the situations we face. I believe God wants to unveil the spirit realm to us and lead us to pray more effectively.

## Our God Rules Over All

We begin to pray more effectively when we remember that our God rules over all. We see this truth demonstrated in many stories in the Old Testament.

In one such story, we find what happens after the enemies of the Israelites made a calculated error. Ben-Hadad, the king of Aram, picked a battle with Israel and lost. His advisors, reexamining the spiritual landscape, said, "Their gods are gods of the hills. That is why they were too strong for us. But if we fight them on the plains, surely we will be stronger than they" (1 Kings 20:23).

This was the error the Arameans made: They believed the God of the Israelites was restricted to a territory and therefore restricted in His ability to deliver His people. However, when the Arameans executed their new strategy, God gave the king of Israel a prophetic word through a prophet. He said, "Because the Arameans think the LORD is a god of the hills and not a god of the valleys, I will deliver this vast army into your hands, and you will know that I am the LORD" (verse 28). Although the Israelite army was much smaller in comparison, the Lord delivered the Arameans into their hands, just as the prophet foretold. God proved to be not only the God of the hills, but also the God of the plains and everything else.

Now, this battle between the Arameans and the Israelites reveals their understanding of the spirit realm. They believed different gods ruled nations and geographical territories. However, the Israelites understood their God ruled over all. These other gods were actually demons[1] and were a constant snare to the Israelites. They are the reason God invoked the commandment, "You shall have no other gods before me" (Exodus 20:3).

Battles between the Israelites and other nations, whether for new territory or their deliverance, then became battles between the God of the Israelites and the gods of the opposing nations. For example, the Lord delivered the Israelites from Egypt by dealing with the gods of Egypt, saying, "On that same night I will pass through Egypt and strike down every firstborn of both people and animals, and I will bring judgment on all the gods of Egypt. I am the LORD" (Exodus 12:12).

Another example can be seen in the battle between David and Goliath. King David, as a young boy, brazenly provoked the Philistine giant to a fight, intending to defeat him. Goliath, insulted by David's young age and size, invoked curses in the name of his god on David and threatened David's life. David responded by saying, "You come against me with sword and spear and javelin, but I come against you in the name of the LORD Almighty, the God of the armies of Israel, whom you have defied" (1 Samuel 17:45).

We know the rest of the story. The God of the Israelites shouted His position by anointing David to win the fight with a slingshot and a rock. Once again, a battle between two people who represented two nations was really a battle that began in the heavenly places.

A parallel spiritual battle rages on today as we advance Christ's rule and authority on the earth. Jesus instructed His disciples to "go and make disciples of all nations" (Matthew 28:19). This instruction was an act of war against the demonic spirits assigned to deceive the nations from worshiping the one true God.

Remember that Satan and his demonic cohorts lost their *authority* to rule at the cross—authority now returned to all those in Christ—but they did not lose their *power*. They will continue their sinister assignments in the heavenly places until overcome by the prayers of the Church. That is where we come in.

Just look at the example of Daniel, another Old Testament figure who teaches us how to contend with the spirits fighting to have their way with us on earth. During the Babylonian exile, the young man Daniel was taken captive and forced to serve King Nebuchadnezzar II of Babylon. King Nebuchadnezzar's religion was downright scary and in conflict with Daniel's Jewish faith. Daniel overcame several life-and-death challenges connected to his worship of Yahweh, and as a result, King Nebuchadnezzar began to acknowledge the greatness of Daniel's God.

Then we find Daniel reading the book of Jeremiah and noticing the prophetic time frame for the release of his people from Babylonian exile (see Daniel 9 and Jeremiah 29:10). Freedom was at hand!

The new Persian ruler, King Cyrus, had released the Jews to go back to Jerusalem, but many chose not to go or were hindered from doing what they set out to do.[2] Daniel needed more understanding of this and turned back to God with prayer, fasting and mourning.

After 21 days of consecration, an angel appeared to him and told him an unusual story. The angel shared that he was dispatched to Daniel from heaven on the first day Daniel prayed, but a demonic spirit prince assigned to the land of Persia had stopped the angel from advancing to reach Daniel. This prince was not human. It was a demon that held back this angel and Daniel's answer to prayer. Finally, an angelic spirit prince named Michael came and fought with the demonic prince of Persia. As a result, Daniel's messenger angel broke through and appeared to Daniel with some real answers about what awaited his people (see Daniel 10:1–21).

This seems like a scene from the movie *The Lord of the Rings*, I know, but it is not. Similar scenes play out again and again in our cities and nations. Those who see into the spirit realm can watch these activities take place but may not know how to navigate them. Even worse, they may see a territorial spirit at work, such as Daniel's prince of Persia, and pronounce in defeat, "There's a demon over this city!"

Heaven is not passive about these entities, but our cooperation in prayer and fasting is needed to see the angels bind and destroy the demonic powers and bring answers from heaven to earth.

## We Have Territorial Enemies

The apostle Paul describes what appears to be an organized hierarchy of beings in the demonic kingdom in the Ephesians 6:12 passage, saying, "For our struggle is not against flesh and blood, but against the rulers, against the authorities, against the powers of this dark world and against the spiritual forces of evil in the heavenly realms." Although there are different theories behind their origin, these beings are most likely fallen angels.

In descending order, let's consider our contending enemies. First, there are the rulers, also translated "principalities" (Greek: *archai*). These are most identifiable as high-ranking spirit princes, such as the prince of Persia and the prince of Greece that were mentioned in the Daniel passage (see Daniel 10:13, 20).

The authorities (Greek: *exousia*) are spirits that stand behind human authorities to oppose the work of God. Consider the centurion in Matthew 8:9, who referred to himself as a man under authority (*exousia*) and a man who exercised authority. Just as people can stand under human authority, human authority can submit to spiritual authority, whether demonic or divine. Elymas the sorcerer, for example, was one who appeared to stand under demonic authority as he attempted to oppose the work of God in order to retain control of Sergius Paulus, the governor, and the island of Patmos (see Acts 13:4–12).

The powers of darkness (Greek: *dunamis*) work culturally and philosophically to bind people groups from seeing the Lord. Examples are false religions, such as Hinduism; philosophies, such as humanism; and political ideologies, such as communism and all other -*isms* that deny the expression of God. James speaks of a kind of wisdom that is demonic (see James 3:15), which is found in belief systems created and promoted by the powers of darkness to blind people's minds to the truth of Jesus Christ.

Finally, the spiritual forces of evil (Greek: *kosmokratoras*) are the lower-ranking spirits that afflict people through infirmity, fear, rebellion, deception, divination, complacency and the like.[3]

We handle higher-ranking spirits and lower-ranking spirits differently, and Jesus shows us what to do by example. When it comes to lower-ranking spirits, we see Him journeying to different towns by the leading of His Father, where He encountered people possessed by various spirits. These spirits would identify themselves either by speaking out to Jesus ("I know who You are!"; see Mark 1:24) or by making other manifestations through the people they afflicted, such as screaming, convulsing or foaming at the mouth (see Mark 1:26; 9:20). Jesus, being anointed of the Spirit to set the oppressed free (see Luke 4:18), would personally command the demons to leave (see Mark 1:25). The disciples continued ministering to the demonically oppressed in this way, and we are to do the same. When we encounter a demon-possessed person and they begin to manifest, we command the demon (or demons) to leave them, in Jesus' name, and they have to go. (See appendix B for a practical guide to casting out demons in your ministry.)

On the other hand, we do not see Jesus address higher-ranking spirits in the same manner. He handled them, but He did so differently. I mention this because of the intercessors I have encountered or read about who take it upon themselves to confront territorial spirits directly—including Satan—in order to "tear them down." I am uncomfortable with this, as they appear to be doing it out of their own will, rather than by a leading of the Spirit.

When it came to addressing Satan, the prince of demons, Jesus only spoke to him after Satan had revealed himself to Jesus during the time of testing in the wilderness. Remember that Jesus was led by the Holy Spirit into the wilderness and did not do this of His own initiative (see Matthew 4:1). He did not even speak on His own but responded to Satan's verbal baiting by quoting the written Word of God (see verses 4, 7 and 10).

What do we learn from this? We learn that when handling higher-ranking spirits, we need to remember we are in partnership with the Holy Spirit. He is an expert Guide when it comes to navigating the spiritual realm. When He leads us into spiritual battle, He will lead us into victory. Without His help, we will not be effective.

I have experienced the differences between higher and lower spirits in my own city and ministry. In one such instance, it was my husband's first year as senior pastor, and he had just finished teaching a Bible study at the church. As we all walked out of the study room, making our way down the hallway, a large man ran up to us. He was shaking and breathing hard, saying, "There's a problem in the sanctuary!"

By now, I was in the front lobby and turned to look inside the sanctuary. I threw on the lights and opened the doors. There, I saw a blonde teenage girl huddled all alone in the area between the seats and the platform.

I stepped inside the aisle and began to make my approach. The nearer I came to her, the stronger I felt them. *Demons!* I could discern there was more than one and that they were occultic in nature.

I tried to speak to the young woman as gently as I could, but she was inaccessible, as the spirits were moving through her.

I said several times, quite forcefully, "In the name of Jesus, I command every one of you to leave her!"

It took about ten minutes, but the evil spirits came out and the young woman came back to herself. Again, just as Jesus did when handling lower-ranking spirits, I addressed the spirits and commanded them to leave. It seemed to be the appropriate and biblical response.

In contrast, I was once led by the Holy Spirit to contend with a specific occultic spirit in our city. This would be an example of contending with a higher-ranking spirit. It was not in possession of a person but was a territorial spirit and "seated" on a portion of land. This battle was completely different and required a much stronger confrontation.

It started not too long after we began praying together as a church once a week. As I led the prayer time, I would feel a viselike grip on my head while praying for our city. Sometimes it was so strong, I wondered if my head was going to explode. I could not explain the source of the feeling but would continue to pray, no matter how oppressive it became. Soon after, we began to fast annually as a church for forty days.

During one of these times of fasting, I began contending with something deeply spiritual and very evil. I did not pick the fight on my own but was led into it. Again, I discerned it was a demonic spirit that was occultic in nature, and I could feel its location in the city. It sat in the north area of Turlock—an area of the city that was undeveloped and mostly fields.

One night I awoke around one or two in the morning, feeling again the severe contention with this spirit and even sensing it could take my life. I do not know how this happened, but as I felt myself struggling to stay alive, it seemed that my spirit left my body in that intense moment and proceeded to travel through five different homes of people in my church. As my spirit entered their homes, I found them in their beds and attempted to wake them, telling them to pray for me because I was in trouble. After I left the fifth home, I came back to my body and continued to contend, but I began to feel a sense of peace. The battle was not over, but I was alive.

I was so sure of what happened during the night that I began to question the families of the five households the following weekend. I asked, "Did you pray for me the other night?" Four households said no. The fifth, however, belonged to a prayerful woman named Veronica Martinez. I asked her the same question. She replied in her beautiful accent, "Oh, yes! Your spirit appeared in my room. I knew I needed to pray for you." I thanked her because her prayer before God probably saved my life.

Toward the end of the forty-day fast, we were at Saturday night prayer, praying for our city. I felt that same severe contention again, but now something was different. I felt a breakthrough and clear victory over that demon. I kicked off my shoes in that moment, a response to the breakthrough I felt in my spirit.

Whenever I go through something like this, I do not settle for what I feel or what I think I see. I begin looking for results. If it is real, something will appear to prove it out.

The first thing I noticed was that the vise grip on my head had stopped and I could pray without oppression. I also noticed a bump in church growth during the next month. The biggest result happened within the next year. The area of land where that spirit was seated came under wide-scale construction and development. The land became useful instead of standing barren. New homes were built, as well as a new school and plenty of shopping areas. We purchased a beautiful new home in that area, too. (To the victor go the spoils, right?)

In hindsight, I realized I should have sought help from like-minded intercessors in this situation. I neglected to do that out of ignorance, and that caused me to suffer more than was necessary.

What I want you to take from these stories is this: When God gives you an assignment, He gives you authority for the assignment. However, even though we have the authority to act, we are not to handle our assignments presumptuously. We do not presume authority over territorial spirits and confront them just for the sake of confronting them. This would be misusing our spiritual authority and could take us outside of God's protection in a dangerous way.

I believe this is what happened to an influential pastor, intercessor and author who once organized a huge prayer crusade in a metropolitan city. During the crusade, he led a stadium full of people to confront the city's demonic powers and principalities. He targeted principalities and powers of occultism and perversion in an attempt to tear them down. Instead of the demonic powers being torn down, however, he appeared to be the one torn down. Within a short time, his reputation was attacked on national television, which affected his ministry. Later, it was reported that he had lost his mind, his marriage and his ministry.

It is important for us to heed the words of John Paul Jackson, from his book *Needless Casualties of War*, where he says, "Jesus showed us the proper way to use authority. He did nothing on His own authority, but only what the Father told Him to do."[4] By operating from this place, we keep from going astray and suffering dire consequences.

Advancing the Kingdom of God does not come without a fight. As we prayerfully commit to His priorities and step out in response to His specific instructions, we will come into contention with territorial spirits as the two kingdoms collide. Prayer becomes our weapon of choice and the only thing that really works.

Whole cities and nations, not just individuals, still suffer the chains of demonic bondage. Intercessors are the ones who become the problem solvers in such circumstances. Intercessors seem to catch the coming winds of revival before anyone else. They are compelled to pray until every spiritual obstacle is re-ordered to accommodate the plans of God. Intercessors invite the presence and power of Jesus into their *metron*, thus stopping Satan's plans, cleansing the atmosphere and putting angels on assignment (see Psalm 103:20). Furthermore, as much as demons resist you, you will discover even greater armies of angels ready to assist you—the subject to which we will now turn.

## Kingdom Prayer Principles

1. When Jesus said to "go and make disciples of all nations" (Matthew 28:19), it was an act of war against the demonic spirits assigned to deceive the nations.

2. Satan and his demonic cohorts lost their authority to rule at the cross. They did not lose their power, however, and will continue their sinister assignments until overcome by the authority and prayers of the Church.

3. When God gives a directive to advance on something and it is met with opposition, we can assume there is a territorial spirit behind it. We need to consider the spirit of the matter since we do not live in a purely natural world.

4. We are citizens of heaven and earth at the same time. Prayer is the place where heaven and earth become one.

5. Because we live in both a natural and a spiritual realm, it is normal for Christians to encounter the spiritual realm in the context of prayer.

6. We experience two kingdoms in conflict and exercise our spiritual authority with higher spirits and lower spirits differently. Lower spirits are often handled personally, while higher spirits are handled as the Spirit leads us.

7. When God gives us an assignment, He gives us authority for the assignment. Even though we have the authority to act, we do not handle our assignments presumptuously.

8. Prayer is our weapon of choice and the only thing that really works. Intercessors seem to catch the coming winds of revival before anyone else. They are compelled to pray until every spiritual obstacle is reordered to accommodate the plans of God.

## Thoughts for Reflection

1. Has God ever given you a directive that did not work out as planned? Why do you think it did not work out?

2. How have you experienced living in both a natural and a spiritual realm at the same time?

3. Have you ever recognized a conflict in your life as having spiritual dimensions behind it? How did you know?

4. Jesus dealt with higher and lower spirits differently. What does that look like in your world?

5. Some people advise others not to be "overly spiritual." Is that possible? Explain why or why not.

# 6

# God's Mighty Invisible Army

Remember Ben-Hadad, king of Aram, whom we discussed in the last chapter—the one who believed God was sovereign only over the hills? Well, we are going to look at yet another time he lost out.

This same king went to war against the king of Israel during the time of Elisha the prophet. But Elisha kept revealing the king of Aram's secret war plans to the king of Israel, thus saving Israel from surprise attacks (see 2 Kings 6:8–10). Ben-Hadad became so frustrated with this that he demanded to know who in his army kept betraying him. He discovered he was not being betrayed from the inside, however, but by the prophet Elisha, who was capable of hearing "the very words [the king spoke] in [his] bedroom" (verse 12).

In response, the king of Aram and his troops surrounded the city where Elisha lived. He intended to kill Elisha so he could go on to conquer Israel, uninterrupted.

As the troops surrounded the city of Dothan, Elisha's servant cried out in fear because death appeared imminent. Elisha, however, was not worried. He could see into the spirit realm. He told his servant, "Those who are with us are more than those who are with them" (verse 16). He then prayed to God that his servant be given eyes to see what he saw. God answered favorably, and the servant's spiritual eyes were opened.

What did he see? Innumerable angelic troops on horses and chariots of fire filling the sky (see verse 17). Soon enough, the battle was over, with Israel as the victor.

### Angels among Us

Everywhere God is and everywhere God's people are, His angels are there, too. We see in both the Old and New Testaments a variety of scenes that point to the reality of angels. They are an invisible army on assignment, helping the Body of Christ fulfill her assignment to preach the Gospel and bring heaven to earth.

If we could see into the spiritual realm and observe where the angels are and what they are doing, we would find peace in the most difficult situations. Sadly, the ministry of angels has been underemphasized. I believe this is because we avoid what we fear and reject what we do not understand. The ministry of angels is a key to answered prayer, though, and therefore something we need to discover and embrace.

So, what do we need to know about angels?

First, that angels are immortal spirits created by God before the earth was formed. We see them giving God the glory as the earth's foundations were laid (see Job 38:4–7). We also note that they are servants and "sent to serve those who will inherit salvation" (Hebrews 1:14). Those who will inherit salvation

82

are us—people on earth—so we can presume angels came into being prior to the arrival of human beings on earth.

The Bible also says there is an innumerable number of angels (see Jeremiah 33:22 NASB; Hebrews 12:22). Although this is not said directly in Scripture, we can put some passages together to discover there are more angels than demons in existence. Lucifer, also known as Satan or the Morning Star, was cast out of heaven to the earth (see Isaiah 14:12; Luke 10:18; Revelation 9:1). That is why we see him show up in the Garden to tempt Adam and Eve. And when Satan fell from heaven, he took a third of the angels with him. The apostle John describes how this happened. He saw a vision of a dragon sweeping a third of the stars from the sky with his tail and then being hurled out of heaven with his angels (see Revelation 12:7–9). This shows us there are probably two angels for every one demon. If God is still inclined to create angels, there could be many more.

Angels inhabit both heaven and earth and actually travel between them. We know this from the story in Genesis 28:10–22, where we find the Lord appearing to Jacob in a dream, telling him of the generational promises coming to him and his family. In the dream, the Lord stood above a stairway that connected heaven and earth. Angels used this stairway to travel back and forth between both places. Jesus later confirmed this detail, telling Nathanael that he would see angels descending between heaven and earth because of the Son of Man, referring to Himself (see John 1:51).

Why do angels go back and forth between heaven and earth? Their primary purpose is to serve God in heaven and to serve the heirs of salvation, which are you and I, believers in Jesus as Lord (see Psalm 103:20; Hebrews 1:14). Angels serve and perform a variety of spiritual and natural tasks. In general, here is what they do:

1. Protect (see Daniel 6:20–23; 2 Kings 6:13–17)
2. Guide (see Mark 16:5–7; Acts 8:26)
3. Reveal information (see Luke 1:11–20; Acts 1:11)
4. Provide (see Genesis 21:17–20; 1 Kings 19:5–7)
5. Arrive in response to prayer (see Daniel 9:22–23; Acts 12:8–12)
6. Fight demonic spirits (see Daniel 10:20; Revelation 12:7)
7. Care for believers upon death (see Luke 16:22; Jude 9)

Many people can cite experiences where they knew an angel had protected them, either because they saw an angel or because the circumstances were too miraculous not to have included the involvement of an angel. For example, a woman in our church was driving on the freeway when the cars stopped much too quickly for her to respond.

"It all seemed like it was happening in slow motion," Catherine says. "I watched myself drive into the car in front of me, pass through the vehicle and even the person inside, and then to a clear space on the road without damage or harm."

Several vehicles in front of and behind Catherine's car were hit in the bottlenecked traffic, but she went untouched. The driver of the car she passed through jumped out of his vehicle in surprise and fright, asking, "What was that?" He knew some type of miracle had happened. This is the work of angels.

Again, relating the story from the last chapter, the prophet Daniel had been fasting and praying for 21 days when an angel appeared to him. The angel said, "Your words were heard, and I have come in response to them" (Daniel 10:12).

Angels are being dispatched from heaven to earth to answer our prayers. Remember, this is being done by permission of our heavenly Father, because all answers to prayer originate in Him.

Prayer puts this invisible army into action. However, there are principles we need to understand.

## Heaven Open to Us

John had just baptized Jesus in the Jordan River. Afterward, Jesus began to pray, and when He did, "heaven was opened" (Luke 3:21). Out of heaven, the Holy Spirit fell upon Him like a dove, and His Father spoke His love for Jesus in the hearing of all the people.

Although this passage does not provide direct instruction, we can receive insight about prayer through it. That insight would be this: When Jesus prayed, heaven opened. If that happened to Jesus, who was our example, then it will happen for us. We will pray, and heaven will open over us, too.

Paul the apostle wrote, "Praise be to the God and Father of our Lord Jesus Christ, who has blessed us in the heavenly realms with every spiritual blessing in Christ" (Ephesians 1:3). Every blessing of God exists first in the heavenly realm. A lifestyle of prayer causes heaven to open over us, and we can expect God's blessings to fall upon us like the rain (see Deuteronomy 28:12).

When heaven opens, we can expect a variety of things to happen. First, we can expect an increase in angelic activity. It is not necessary to see angels to verify this, but we can trust the biblical pattern either way. The angels will ascend and descend on the location where we have prayed (see Genesis 28:10–12; John 1:51). We can also expect the Holy Spirit to fall upon us in power. When the 120 believers gathered to pray in the Upper Room, heaven opened and the Holy Spirit fell upon them in response to their prayers (see Acts 2:1–4). An open heaven is also connected to provision and our needs being met. Asaph described in the Psalms how heaven opened and manna, or "angel's food," came down (see Psalm 78:23–25). Malachi also instructed the people to restore their tithes to see the windows of heaven open up again over their lives (see Malachi 3:10). Finally, an open heaven allows us to experience the voice and revelation of God in ways we normally would not. The apostle John stood before an open door in heaven and heard a voice that invited him, saying, "Come up here, and I will show you what must take place after this" (Revelation 4:1).

When the blessings of heaven are not falling on our lives, we need to check the conditions of heaven. If you are sensitive to spiritual atmospheres, an open or closed heaven is an atmosphere you can feel. A closed heaven feels like your prayers hit the ceiling and fall back down. This verse describes it well: "The sky over your head will be bronze, the ground beneath you iron" (Deuteronomy 28:23). In the context of this verse, heaven closes when the people of God fail to hear and obey God's voice.

Heaven can also be hindered by darkness above. Again in the story of Daniel, heaven was closed because a demonic prince, the prince of Persia, stood in his way. It opened again only after the archangel Michael fought and won against this spirit, which released Daniel's answer to prayer.

Heaven is not always open, which means angels are not always on assignment to help. The prophet Isaiah seemed to shout in frustration, "Oh, that you would rend the heavens and come down!" (Isaiah 64:1). If we read further in the passage, we see the Israelites had stopped praying and were experiencing the consequences of their sins. Prayerlessness keeps heaven closed, which blocks God's angels and blessings from reaching us.

For us, Jesus has now become the "open heaven," which is characterized by perpetual angelic activity (see John 1:51). We step into an open heaven the same way Jesus did: when we pray.

We pray to our heavenly Father in Jesus' name, asking for His will to be done on earth as it is in heaven. This puts us in direct proximity to the angels coming and going between earth and heaven, having come in response to our prayers and with our prayers putting them on assignment in earth's realm.

## Authority within Us

While I was ministering at Greater Chicago Church in the Oak Park area, a whole new world opened to me in this regard. Pastors Ian and Rachel Carroll asked me to do a comprehensive seminar on prayer. At the first session, I communicated to the attendees about God's ability to pour out His Spirit on the entire city of Chicago.

Perhaps that sounds grandiose, but I based it on an incredible outpouring that took place while I attended Oral Roberts University. In 1993, the Holy Spirit fell on the entire campus for a month in a glorious visitation. During that time, the Holy Spirit did not have much regard for what people were doing and seemed to enjoy interrupting chapel services, classrooms, the cafeteria, the outdoors, the library, restrooms . . . everything, everywhere! Students were often found holding on to poles, chairs and trees and acting quite drunk in His presence (see Acts 2:13, 15). It was a life-changing and unforgettable experience.

As I shared this story with the audience in Chicago, the room's atmosphere changed. A band of angels came into the room, and their presence stopped anything else from happening. I have the ability to see into the spirit realm and saw the angels come in that moment, but you did not need to see them to experience the results. They were quite eager and lively in their behavior. They came in all shapes and sizes, and the wings of some hit me as they moved back and forth in the room.

I kept waiting for them to settle down so I could finish what I was saying. But they simply would not settle down.

Angels carry the glory of God, and the glory began to fall in the room. It caused an eruption of uncontrolled laughter by the attendees and me. I call this kind of laughter "inexpressible and glorious joy" (1 Peter 1:8).

I kept wondering what the pastors thought of all of this. I finally gave up and turned the service back to Ian. He led all of us in prayer for Chicago, which seemed to be the most appropriate thing to do.

After the service ended, I asked Ian about this activity, and he said it was a regular occurrence with guest speakers. Ian can also see into the spirit realm and has an uncommon connection with angels. He explained to me, "These angels are on assignment for Chicago." He further clarified that angels would show up at these particular meetings and activate around certain phrases related to their mission. What stirred them, apparently, were key words or phrases, like *revival* or *outpouring* or *Chicago*. He said I lasted on the platform longer than most speakers, but it was always the same scenario. These angels would come in their overwhelming glory, and this would stop the meeting and turn it into a glory service. It was truly beautiful, and I could see where one would want to live in that all day long.

The following morning, I woke up and found angels all around me. I could see them and hear them talking. They were just as excited as the night before, but I discerned[1] by the Holy Spirit that we were not going in the same direction. I felt from the Lord that I was there to put a sustaining word into this church. Greater Chicago Church needed my story and my principles to aid them through future obstacles. If the angels interrupted the teaching again, it would not be helpful in the long term.

Spontaneously, right there in the room where I had been sleeping, I called a meeting with these spirit beings. I had never thought to do that before, but it just came out of my mouth.

I said, "Angels! I'm here to put the sustaining word in this church so they can last and not become a casualty. They have obstacles up ahead, and I have the keys. You need to let me teach and prove the word with signs. When I'm done, you can do what you want."

I could feel them come into alignment, and I felt a sense of order materialize.

Their presence was still there at the church as I spoke that day and the next, but at this point we were on the same page with each other. They would get active during the right times, even providing miraculous signs, but allowed me to retain the lead. For example, as I prayed for the group to receive an anointing to see into the spirit realm (see 2 Kings 6:17), one woman received even more than that. She was healed instantly of nearsightedness and no longer needed her glasses. This miracle raised the faith level of the room to receive the anointing for spiritual sight.

Some might call what I did with the angels in that spontaneous meeting quenching the Spirit, but it is really connected to our priestly and kingly roles on earth (see Revelation 5:10). Angels are not on their own charge. They are assigned to serve humans, not the other way around (see Hebrews 1:14). They remain mighty and powerful by nature, but we are still the earth's leaders (see Psalm 115:16).

I have heard and read much counsel from Christian leaders not to worship angels. Given the practices of some Catholics, Wiccans, pagans and those in New Age cults, this counsel is understandable. Those religions often pray to angels or seek them out in ways that are not biblical. The instruction not to worship angels, however, is often misheard as "Don't work with angels" or "Don't talk to them." Angels are not off-limits to us. Within biblical boundaries, we can ask the Father for them and work with them.

## Ask the Father

When it comes to asking the Father for angels, consider what happened in the Garden of Gethsemane on the night Jesus was arrested. Judas, one of the twelve disciples, had just betrayed Jesus. As the officers came to arrest Jesus, Peter drew his sword and cut off the ear of the high priest's servant. Jesus healed the man's ear but swiftly rebuked Peter for resorting to violence. He said, "Do you think I cannot call on my Father, and he will at once put at my disposal more than twelve legions of angels?" (Matthew 26:53).

This is another one of those passages that is not giving direct instruction but still provides insight into the things we can ask of our heavenly Father. Jesus could ask for armies of angels to assist Him, if needed. And if He could ask for angels, then we can ask for them, too. We can ask the Father to send them on assignment to us for things we know they already do: protect, fight, guide, provide and so on. Notice that Jesus did not ask for the angels to come that day, because it was not the will of His Father that He be saved from the cross. Asking the Father for angels needs to be done in alignment with the Word of God and the will of God.

## Negotiate Details

During his residency in Sodom and Gomorrah, Lot received two angels into his home (see Genesis 19). The angels had come on assignment from God to rescue Lot and his family before God destroyed the city for its abominable wickedness. The angels gave Lot specific instructions: "Flee for your lives! Don't look back, and don't stop anywhere in the plain! Flee to the mountains or you will be swept away!" (verse 17).

Lot had a different idea, however.

"I can't flee to the mountains," he said. "Look, here is a town near enough to run to, and it is small. Let me flee to it. . . . Then my life will be spared" (verses 19–20).

Lot understood that staying in Sodom and Gomorrah was not an option. However, he perceived his destination was negotiable, and the angels accepted Lot's change of plans. This means that when we operate within the will of God, we can still negotiate details with the angels who come to give us aid.

To coincide with this idea, I once heard the story of a young revivalist who had contracted a terrible fever while overseas on a ministry trip. The fever killed him, and angels appeared to take him home to heaven. He resisted the angels several times, however, unwilling to leave. At the same time, other ministers had gathered to pray him back to life. The angels finally let him go, and he lived to tell the tale.

### Loose Them

Jesus gave us the keys of the kingdom of heaven—keys, meaning authority. He said, "I will give you the keys of the kingdom of heaven; whatever you bind on earth will be bound in heaven, and whatever you loose on earth will be loosed in heaven" (Matthew 16:19). Many of us understand this to mean we are to bind the devil and his demons. To *bind* something means "to tie it up," and we accomplish that by making a specific command with our words (see Mark 11:23–24).

At the same time, Jesus also gave us the power to loose things. What do we have the power to loose? Angels. We loose the angels the same way we bind demons: by using our words. For one thing, we are charged with making known the will of God in the presence of the angels (see Ephesians 3:10). Angels also listen for and obey the word of the Lord (see Psalm 103:20). The word of the Lord comes from Jesus Himself in heaven or through His Church on earth. We also call that a prophetic word. Our prophetic words are heard and observed by angels and will put them on assignment.

We see this in the life of King David. He made a command not only to all of creation, but also to the angels: "Praise the LORD" (Psalm 148:1; see also verse 2). Jacob, too, wrestled with an angel all night and refused to let the angel go, eventually making a command: "I will not let you go unless you bless me" (Genesis 32:26).

I have experienced this in my own way. During my first pregnancy, I became very ill in the middle of the night and could not hold anything down. An angel appeared, and I spoke to it. I said, "Lay your hand on my stomach, and I will be healed." The angel did exactly that, and I was instantly well.

Just as there are demons that afflict us with sickness (see Luke 13:10–17), there are angels that act as healing agents to us. At the end of the day, however, all healing comes from God, and we are to credit Him, not the angels, with the healing we receive.

### Remain in the Word of God

When working with angels, understand that they strictly uphold the Word of God. Not to do so would be rebellion with severe punishment. Remember the example of Lucifer and all his fallen angels with him: "And the angels who did not keep their positions of authority but abandoned their proper dwelling—these he has kept in darkness, bound with everlasting chains for judgment on the great Day" (Jude 6). To be flippant, casual or careless with the angels will, at best, get you ignored. At worst, it could bring a strict penalty, and we need to be aware of that possibility.

For example, Gabriel appeared to Zechariah the priest with a message from God. He told Zechariah he would have a son and to name him John. Zechariah did not believe the angel, and when he voiced his unbelief, Gabriel imposed a temporary injunction against him. Zechariah could not physically speak until the birth of his son, John, just as the angel foretold (see Luke 1:5–23, 57–66).

We find another instance of a strict penalty coming against those who do not uphold the will of God in the ministry of Zechariah's son, also known as John the Baptist. John grew to adulthood and fulfilled his assignment to "prepare the way for the Lord" (Mark 1:3). He also challenged Herod Antipas over his sin of adultery, as Herod had married his brother's wife. Herod imprisoned John in response, and his wife made sure to have John executed. Later, Herod appeared before the people of Tyre and Sidon, who worshiped him as a god and not a man. But because Herod did not give God the glory, an angel struck him down and he was eaten by worms and died (see Acts 12:20–23).

Jesus exhorts us and solemnly warns us in regard to the angels: "I tell you, whoever publicly acknowledges me before others, the Son of Man will also acknowledge before the angels of God. But whoever disowns me before others will be disowned before the angels of God" (Luke 12:8–9). Jesus is saying here that if we deny Him or His Word (which is the same as denying Him), the angels will not work with us.

Instead, we need to be like Mary. When the angel Gabriel appeared to her to announce she would become pregnant and give birth to the Son of God, she responded well. "I am the Lord's servant," she answered. "May your word to me be fulfilled" (Luke 1:38).

Working with angels within biblical parameters is not the same as worshiping angels or praying to angels. Angels are of the same classification of being as demon spirits, only they have chosen to remain sinless before God and are assigned to assist us. Someone might ask, "Why do we need to ask for angels? Aren't they rather automated in their function?" Again, we should not assume the will and benefits of God happen without our participation. We can be intentional within our assignments to ensure, like Elisha and his servant found, there are more with us than there are with them.

## Kingdom Prayer Principles

1. There is an invisible army on assignment, helping the Body of Christ.
2. If we could see into the spirit realm and observe what the angels are doing, we would find peace in the most difficult situations.
3. Angels were created as servants and are sent to those who will inherit salvation.
4. There is an innumerable number of angels. There are not as many demons.
5. Angels are dispatched from heaven to earth in response to our prayers.
6. When we pray, heaven opens. An open heaven is characterized by an increase of angelic activity.
7. Within biblical boundaries, we can ask our heavenly Father to send angels, and we can work with them.

## Thoughts for Reflection

1. Have you ever been aware of angels working in your life? If so, what do you believe they were doing?

2. Are you sensitive to spiritual atmospheres? Can you sense the difference between an open heaven and a closed heaven? Have you ever experienced a closed heaven shifting into an open one?

3. Do you ever ask your heavenly Father for His angels to come? What do you ask His angels to do?

4. What does spiritual authority in connection to the angels look like in your world? What evidence do you have that angels are being put on assignment through you?

# 7

# Prophetic Intercession

Joshua, born a slave in Egypt, experienced firsthand the wonders of God's deliverance. He had watched the water turn to blood, the miracle invasions of frogs and insects, the death of all the firstborn in Egypt and the parting of the Red Sea, just to name a few. Was there anything God could not do?

These events built audacious faith in the heart of Joshua. He was ready to go after anything God said he could have.

On the borders of the Promised Land, however, disaster struck. It was the disaster of unbelief. Unbelief in this miracle-working God kept an entire nation out of the land of promise. But in the midst of this contradiction, Joshua did not flinch, and he did not lose heart. Joshua, now Moses' assistant, trusted and waited on God for forty years through the wilderness.

Finally, it was time to move out. Joshua had received his divine orders to take the new generation into the Promised Land. It was a promise that required them to fight for new territory.

Now full of faith, they went to war against the inhabitants and took the land, one city at a time.

The king of Jerusalem, Adoni-Zedek, and his people were alarmed. These Israelite invaders defeated strong cities, one after the other, and seemed invincible. Even the city of Gibeon, an important city full of good fighters, had made a peace treaty with Joshua to become Israel's ally. So Adoni-Zedek appealed to the nearby Amorite kings, and they joined forces to fight against Gibeon.

The Gibeonites made a plea to Joshua for help.

"Come up to us quickly and save us!" they said. "Help us, because all the Amorite kings from the hill country have joined forces against us" (Joshua 10:6).

Joshua prepared his best fighting men to march all night toward the incoming armies.

Along the way, God gave Joshua a sure promise: "Do not be afraid of them; I have given them into your hand. Not one of them will be able to withstand you" (verse 8).

At daybreak, Joshua and his army took the Amorites by surprise. The Lord helped Joshua by throwing the Amorites into confusion and raining killer hailstones on them as they tried to run away.

Joshua knew he would win the battle, but he needed more daylight to do it. The sun was going down, so Joshua did what had never been done before. In the presence of the Lord, he made this declaration before the people of Israel: "Sun, stand still over Gibeon, and you, moon, over the Valley of Aijalon" (verse 12).

Joshua commanded the sun!

These words were the words of Joshua, and yet God honored them as if they were His own. The sun stood still for almost a full day, and Joshua finished off the Amorites, just as God promised he would.

## The Power of a Word

This story illustrates what prophetic intercession looks like. Joshua spoke to the sun, but he was also speaking to the Lord. Look at the words that precede what he said in verse 12: "Joshua *said to the* LORD in the presence of Israel: 'Sun, stand still over Gibeon . . .'" (emphasis added).

Prophetic intercession is a sharp and powerful form of prayer that is communicated as a prophetic word. It is different from asking the Lord to do something, which would be a prayer of petition. Instead, it commands something to be done and puts the invisible realm into motion to bring it to pass.

God respects this type of prayer, as it reflects who He is. He is the Word, and everything came into existence because He spoke it out. He said many times in Genesis 1, "Let there be . . . ," and there was. Kenneth Copeland says in his book *The Power of the Tongue*, "God's words produce exactly what He says. . . . Once He speaks, His words will come to pass."[1] When we understand the power of the word to create, we will better understand the power of prophetic intercession.

The Bible describes the word of God to be alive, active and sharper than any two-edged sword (see Hebrews 4:12). These are not metaphors but real truths about the nature of God's word. His word can pierce through the hardest heart and turn the most difficult situation around. With a word, God caused Abraham and Sarah to have a son when they were past the age of childbearing. With a word, God stopped the rain and then restarted it through the prophet Elijah.

God created everything with a word. There is not anything made that was not made through His word (see John 1:1–3; Hebrews 11:3). God can never speak a lie (see Hebrews 6:18). It is impossible for Him to do so, because of His immutable nature as both the Word and Creator. When He speaks, He creates. When He commands, it stands fast (see Psalm 33:9; 148:5).

His Word holds everything in the universe together, and all creation responds to His Word (see Colossians 1:17). The Bible says, "He sent out his word and healed them" (Psalm 107:20). The disciples were amazed when they realized, "Even the winds and the waves obey him!" (Matthew 8:27).

His Word is living and creates new life in us. We become re-created when we receive Jesus into our hearts. Jesus is God's Word, having come in the flesh (see John 1:14). Because of His Word, referring to Jesus, we become a new creation; the old passes away, and we become new (see 2 Corinthians 5:17).

Furthermore, when it comes to prophetic intercession, it is important to note that the first thing to which God spoke in Genesis was the chaos and the darkness (see Genesis 1:3). The literal Hebrew says, "God said, 'Light, be'; and light was." Jesus, the Word, is described as the Light shining in the darkness, with the darkness unable to overcome it (see John 1:5).

The Bible describes the nature of the prophetic word in a similar way. It is "a light shining in a dark place" (2 Peter 1:19). In prophetic intercession, we prophesy to the dark, chaotic places and command God's light and order to come.

## The Definition of a Prophetic Word

If we are going to prophesy well, we need to understand what a prophetic word is and what it is not. Generally speaking, to *prophesy* is to say what God says. When we say what God says, there is power in those words to bring something to life, for "He is . . . the God who gives life to the dead and calls into being things that were not" (Romans 4:17).

A prophetic word, then, is not just ordinary words or an eloquent statement. The breath of God is on it, making it a "living" word that we send out with authority to accomplish a specific purpose (see Isaiah 55:11). As Christ's representatives on the earth, we are commissioned to speak forth and distribute His words to people and to the spirit realm. It is as Paul teaches: "His [God's] intent was that now, through the church, the manifold wisdom of God should be made known to the rulers and authorities in the heavenly realms" (Ephesians 3:10).

The gift and ability to prophesy is available to all those who believe in Christ. Peter reiterated the promise of the prophet Joel on the Day of Pentecost, saying, "In the last days, God says, I will pour out my Spirit on all people. Your sons and daughters will prophesy" (Acts 2:17). God does not withhold the ability to prophesy from those who desire it. Instead, you prophesy in proportion to your faith. The word *proportion* refers to a ratio. Depending on the size, or ratio, of your faith, you might prophesy in prayer to a neighborhood or city, or you might prophesy to a bigger entity, such as a nation.

The gift of prophecy is a multidimensional gift. It operates in many different contexts and in many different forms. These include personal and corporate (church) prophecy; prophetic artisans and psalmists, such as Bezalel and Asaph (see Exodus 31:2–5; 1 Chronicles 25:2); prophetic teaching and preaching; spiritual seeing and visions; and dreams. The ability to prophesy is not restricted to prophets, either. It is for everyone in the Body of Christ.

## The Types of Prophetic Words

Here, we are going to discuss prophecy in the context of intercession. When you prophesy in prayer, you speak something out in the form of a command. There are several forms this can take.

## A Promise from the Written Word

The first is a promise we speak from the Scriptures.

For example, some years back, as a five-year-old, my son was struggling with harassing fear and anxiety. The Bible says fear is a spirit, so we handled it from that perspective. For an entire year, I prophesied this Scripture to him and over him in prayer: "For God has not given us a spirit of fear, but of power and of love and of a sound mind" (2 Timothy 1:7 NKJV). The fear finally broke off him, and he's been normal ever since. I have since expanded the use of this verse to prophesy over pastors, churches and congregations bound by the spirit of fear.

You can do the same. When you encounter a problem, you can utilize clear promises in the written Word to "legislate" your case in the courts of heaven.

## A Word God Gives Us

On his blog, minister and intercessor Dutch Sheets once shared that he received the Scripture of Isaiah 22:22 from the Lord as a prophetic word, with over forty confirmations. The passage says, "I will place on his shoulder the key to the house of David; what he opens no one can shut, and what he shuts no one can open."

Dutch began to prophesy various decrees to the American government based on this Scripture. A *decree* is "an official order given by a person with power or by a government." As Job 22:28 says, "Thou shalt also decree a thing, and it shall be established" (KJV). He also reclaimed the notion of "An Appeal to Heaven," based on the historical flag of an evergreen tree commissioned by George Washington to be flown throughout the original thirteen American colonies. He said God gave him this phrase and historical backdrop so he could prophesy and make "an appeal to heaven" for the third Great Awakening in America.

Prophetic intercessors find themselves in these types of journeys as the Holy Spirit unveils a directive, a specific word of the Lord, to be prophesied in the context of prayer. Like Dutch, they are awakened to a clue through a divinely ordered set of circumstances. As they dig for meaning, the clue becomes a message and a sure promise of victory as they speak it forth.

### A Word from Our Heart

Just like Joshua, we will have moments when we prophesy in prayer out of the context of our own hearts. Here is what qualifies this to be honored in heaven and then loosed on earth. Jesus said, "If you remain in me and my words remain in you, ask whatever you wish, and it will be done for you" (John 15:7).

One of the first instructions given to Joshua from the Lord was for him to meditate on God's Word day and night in order that he might see success (see Joshua 1:8). Joshua must have done what the Lord required, for look at the success he had.

When we abide in Jesus and His Word, we can prophesy out of the reserve of our own heart, knowing it will reflect His heart and will be done by our heavenly Father.

### A Prophetic Act

A prophetic act is an act of intercession given to you by the Holy Spirit that becomes a sign and a decree to the spirit realm. God starts it, but you act on it, creating the heaven-to-earth connection.

We see prophetic acts all throughout the Bible. The most notable is found in Exodus 12, as the Israelite families killed lambs and put the blood of the lambs on their doorposts. When the death angel came to enact judgment on the region, it passed over all the households covered by the blood. This was a powerful act and a timeless statement.

God is still doing prophetic acts today, but we have to stay in step with what He is doing. We do not put together our own thing or do what someone else has done, just for the sake of doing it. Prophetic acts are powerful visual commands that put the spirit realm into motion once we have heard the Lord.

Bill Johnson, from Bethel Church in Redding, California, once said, "Our words become worlds." God's words in the mouths of His men and women will resurrect dead things to life and birth answers to impossible situations.

## The Ways God Speaks

At the center of prophetic intercession is a genuine heart-to-heart partnership with God to see His will done on earth as in heaven. However, we can determine and prophesy His will only to the degree that we know Him and recognize His voice.

Remember, God is a communicator. He is the Word, and speaking is His nature. But we often miss His voice because we do not understand how God speaks.

God will speak in a variety of ways (see Hebrews 1:1). I once heard prophet and minister Bobby Conner emphasize, "God will speak to you any way He wants to!" I understood this to mean we should not put limits on how God wants to speak with us. As you grow in relationship with Him, you will discover He speaks in many different "spiritual languages." Let's consider some of them now.

### His Written Word

In 2 Timothy 3:16, we find that all Scripture is God-breathed. His written Word is a continuous voice to us for all of life and gives us a framework to hear His voice in other ways. You will learn to recognize God's voice because it will sound like something you already read in the written Word. At the same time, as you read His Word, there will be times when He breathes on a verse or a passage and it seems to shout at you. There will be a burst of life on it. When that happens, know that God is speaking to you in a personal way.

## A Flow of Impressions

Mark Virkler, in his book *Four Keys to Hearing God's Voice*, describes the voice of God as a series of flowing thoughts and flowing pictures.[2] This connects with the words of Jesus, when He said, "Whoever believes in me, as Scripture has said, rivers of living water will flow from within them" (John 7:38).

What this means is that you will often hear the voice of God by paying attention to your inner thoughts and to the pictures that pop into your imagination in the context of prayer. These are often clues about something God is trying to reveal to you. Ask Him why you are thinking about and seeing these thoughts and pictures. You will often be pleasantly surprised at what He reveals to you.

## Dreams

I've heard it said that the nighttime hours allow God to speak to us without interruption. It is as the book of Job relates: "In a dream, in a vision of the night, when deep sleep falls on people as they slumber in their beds, he may speak in their ears" (Job 33:15–16).

Dreams come from different places and for different reasons, but God definitely uses dreams as a vehicle to communicate what He is doing. Concerning the birth of Jesus, Joseph was instructed several times through dreams about what to do. The apostle Paul received instruction in a dream to go and minister to the city of Macedonia (see Acts 16:9–10). My husband has received direction in dreams regarding church situations that needed answers.

Dreams can be a little hard to understand, but if we ever lack wisdom, we can ask God for it, and He promises to give it (see James 1:5). A dream is always an invitation for dialogue with the Lord, and many times it can lead to a season of prophetic intercession.

## Visions

God is releasing His voice in the form of visions to His people. Visions are often multidimensional and come as inward visions; outer visions, like a movie being played on a screen out in front of you; or through a trance, such as what Peter experienced in Acts 10. I have experienced many forms of visions, and it is one of the strongest ways God speaks to me.

For example, I was unable to have children for some time and was praying for God to open my womb. He answered me with a vision. I saw a little boy running around my home, and I knew in my heart his name was David. I did not get pregnant, however, until I prophesied His will to be done. I actually commanded David to come! Soon after, I became pregnant with a boy, and we named him David.

## Nature

I have a friend, Tom Hammond, who receives a recurring sign involving birds. He believes it is connected to the ministry of angels in his life, and he experiences much angelic visitation, too. He cannot leave doors or windows open in his home because birds will fly in. Once, he even had a bird fly to his shoulder and remain there as he took his walk. A few days before he and his family left our campus parsonage to go to Brazil as missionaries, the tree in his front yard was invaded with hundreds of very loud white birds. That was an unforgettable sight!

I have three other friends who receive a similar recurring sign involving owls. For them, it means they need to "wise up" and discern well. I have never once seen an owl, but these friends see them frequently and in various places.

Now, these are not all the ways God speaks. He can speak through other people, through angels, through a still, small voice, through an audible voice, and in even more ways that stretch our imaginations. We will recognize His voice better as we immerse ourselves in His written Word.

We are also admonished to test everything and to hold on to what is good (see 1 Thessalonians 5:21). One way to test what God is saying is to look for confirmation. He is faithful to confirm His word through two or three witnesses (see 2 Corinthians 13:1). Barbara Wentroble, who authored the book *Prophetic Intercession*, said, "The nature of our hearing is imperfect. We don't even hear others clearly."[3] With that in mind, we always want to get input from our pastors and spiritual leaders when God speaks to us, in order to help us with our hearing.

As we learn to hear God's voice, we will also learn the ebb and flow of the river. I am referring to the river that comes from the Holy Spirit that flows out of our hearts (John 7:38). We learn when He is moving and when He is not moving. We discern when He is stirring things up and when He is quieting things down. We learn to flow in His timing and to prophesy the appointed times and seasons in the context of prayer.

## The Appointed Time

Speaking of times and seasons, prophetic intercessors watch over and steward the times and seasons within their spiritual assignments. The prophet Habakkuk shows us how: "I will stand my watch and station myself on the ramparts; I will look to see what he will say to me" (Habakkuk 2:1). When Habakkuk positioned himself to hear the Lord about his assignment, the Lord responded: "Write down the revelation and make it plain on tablets so that a herald may run with it. For the revelation awaits an appointed time" (verses 2–3).

An appointed time is a fixed time. It is like having an appointment on a calendar, only God sets the time and we cannot alter it. For example, God said to Abraham, "I will surely return to you about this time next year, and Sarah your wife will have a son" (Genesis 18:10). Abraham and Sarah had tried to rush God's appointed time, taking matters into their own hands and having Ishmael by Hagar. That did not change God's appointed time, however. God communicated to Abraham the correct timing.

God actively works out His purposes over chronological time, but God, who sits outside of time, will then interrupt chronological time to release His appointed season. Prophetic intercessors will hear from the Lord about God's upcoming appointments. In partnership with Him, they will prophesy to heaven and earth the onset of these appointed seasons.

In the book of Haggai, for example, the remnant Israelites did not believe it was time to rebuild the house of the Lord. They built their own houses but neglected the Lord's house and did so to their detriment. God then spoke the appointed time to the prophet Haggai: It was now time to rebuild the house of the Lord! Haggai acted on that word and initiated a new season with the people. The people stepped into the appointed time of the Lord and rebuilt the temple as Haggai stood by, encouraging them to be strong and work.

I have seen the way these appointed times can work. In one instance, the Holy Spirit gave me a vision about the mayor in my city at the time. He had served in his position for nearly two decades and had a good reputation. I held no complaint about his conduct or decisions, nor did anyone else that I knew of. I want to clarify that, as sometimes we have visions based on our own biases, and it is important to have a clean heart before we act on such things.

The vision I received looked like a mini-movie that took over my imagination for a few seconds and then would repeat itself. In the movie, I watched myself walk over to City Hall, take off my watch and then throw it to the ground. Once I did that, I would proclaim a blessing to the mayor and an end to his assignment.

Since I had never moved a government person out of office before with a prophetic act, I decided to bring a few people to witness it. After a prayer service, I walked over to City Hall with a church boardmember and his wife and conducted the "departure ceremony" just as I had seen it in the vision. A few weeks later, the local newspaper issued a report that the mayor would not be seeking another reelection. The Holy Spirit was calling for a new season in our local government, and I was given the task to prophetically usher in the appointed time.

Prophetic intercessors need to discern the right prophetic word for the right time. The third chapter of Ecclesiastes gives us a list of fourteen opposites with an instruction that there is a season and time for everything. What is the point of this passage? The point is that the right word for one season is the wrong word in another season. For example, there are seasons when we are to build and other seasons when we are to tear down. In some seasons we are called to fight, and other seasons we are to rest.

Prophetic intercessors prophesy the new word for the new season and get things moving in the spirit realm. As prophetic intercessors, how do we know what season it is? The One who holds the key to time is the Holy Spirit, and He faithfully partners with His intercessors to reveal what time it is. As we learn the river of His timing, prophesying it forth in intercession, we also learn when and how to press in for spiritual breakthrough.

## The Lord of the Breakthrough

In ministry and in life, you will have times that you feel you are up against a wall and cannot reach something God has promised to you. Prophetic intercession becomes the sharp sword of God's word that pierces through spiritual barricades to release what God has promised you.

A *breakthrough* is the "act or instance of breaking through an obstacle." We see this demonstrated for us in the story of King David's triumph over the Philistines. When this battle threat rose up, David inquired of the Lord, and God assured him of victory (see 2 Samuel 5:19). David attacked them and won. When David defeated them, he named the place Baal Perazim, which literally means "Lord of the breakthrough." Although David fought the war on the ground, he knew the battle was the Lord's. God had broken through the wall of the enemy.

Many times, prophetic intercession becomes the piercing sword of the Spirit to overcome a spiritual enemy that restricts us. This is the prophetic word of intercession that brings a breakthrough and a turnaround in the most difficult situations. I have participated in this aspect of prophetic intercession on different levels. Let me share with you a story, although not typical, that illustrates how prophetic intercession can bring about a breakthrough.

It was 2002, and we had just introduced our church to the gift of prophecy. We were using training materials from Kris Vallotton to activate and teach people how to walk in this gift so they could prophesy to others. It was well received, with many from the church participating in the training. I was amazed to see people ministering in depths they had never experienced before.

A year into this new ministry, I had a very disturbing dream. It was about a blonde woman who was holding a small white dog. In the dream, she had kidnapped my son. The intensity of the dream made me feel as though something was wrong, but I did not understand why.

The next day, I went about my normal business and happened to arrive at the place where the dream had its setting. As I walked into a place of business, I noticed a woman holding the same dog I had seen in the dream. It was not the same woman, but it was definitely the same dog. Now I was sure something was wrong.

The following three years were unbelievable. I had never experienced so much accusation, backstabbing, contention or rejection from people, many of whom were close to me. Our prophetic ministry began receiving unfounded accusations in our church from all directions. I also became ill with a chemical imbalance.

The last summer before this got turned around, I was invited to teach a workshop at the Bethel School of the Prophets in Redding, California. It was rough getting there. My husband had contracted viral pneumonia a few weeks prior, and I was still in the throes of my chemical imbalance. However, I was determined to go.

I had a great week at the school and came home very encouraged. That Saturday, I went to our prayer chapel to pray on my own for a few hours before the evening prayer service. I was in good spirits and entered into prayer happy and peaceful. Then, as I began to worship, the atmosphere took a sudden shift. I could tell I was dealing with a strong demonic power, the strongest I had ever encountered.

Words of judgment began to flow out of my mouth, something I had never done or heard anyone do before. My words were not nearly as poetic as those spoken by the Old Testament prophets when they pronounced their judgments, but what fueled my words felt similar, and I could feel the power underneath them.

"You're done," I declared. "I am destroying you. I'm taking you out!"

I called our associate pastor's wife, Bernice Hammond, to come to the church and pray with me. We prayed, and then I asked her a question without knowing why.

"Have you had any dreams lately?" I asked.

"Yes," she said. "But I don't want to tell you."

I encouraged her to share it.

She hesitated and then responded, "I dreamed you hired a hit man to kill a blonde woman!"

When she said that, I knew in my heart what was going on and had a sense of what to do about it. We left the chapel and drove to the location depicted in the dream three years ago. As we stood in the middle of the field, I looked up to the sky and shouted out the prophetic word: "Release the angel"—in other words, the hit man—"to destroy the Jezebel spirit, in the name of Jesus!"

Bernice and I are both prophetic seers and could hardly believe what we then saw in the spirit realm. We watched an angel come and destroy the Jezebel spirit that had been warring against me. The Bible says the saints will worship God with a sword in their hand and execute the written judgment (see Psalm 149:6–9).

Bernice and I drove back to the prayer service, which was now almost over. We told the attendees what had happened and ended up praying together outside. As we were praying, the Lord gave us another sign of victory: The ground began to shake under our feet, and we could all feel it (see Acts 4:31).

I went home that night and told Ron everything that had happened. I continued to hear much activity in the spirit realm in connection to the breakthrough. I perceived that very night that we were finally out of the rough season and were in a new place of spiritual authority. Sure enough, the church began to see an increase in salvations, healings and deliverances. What was most notable was the increase in deliverances, a sign of the increase of authority we had just received (see Revelation 2:26).

The complexities of the spirit realm mystify all of us at times. Yet in all circumstances, God remains the Lord of the breakthrough. Prophetic intercession opens the spirit realm to us so we can prophesy in prayer more intelligently. Even so, we will encounter unyielding circumstances that seem to be untouchable. There is an answer in God, but we need to find the right key. That is the point at which we need to add fasting to our prayers, because fasting is a game changer. Let's turn to the power of fasting next.

## Kingdom Prayer Principles

1. Prophetic intercession is a sharp and powerful prayer communicated as a prophetic word.
2. When we understand the power of the word to create, we will better understand the power of prophetic intercession.

3. In prophetic intercession, we prophesy to the dark, chaotic places and command God's light and order to come.

4. We can determine and prophesy God's will only to the degree that we know Him and recognize His voice.

5. As we learn to hear God's voice, we will also learn the ebb and flow of the "river." We learn to flow in His timing and prophesy the appointed times and seasons in the context of prayer.

6. Prophetic intercession becomes the sharp sword of God's word that pierces through spiritual barricades to release what God has promised us.

7. Prophetic intercession opens the spirit realm to us so we can prophesy in prayer more intelligently.

## Thoughts for Reflection

1. What is your response to the gift of prophecy that flows in tangent with intercession? Have you ever prophesied in the context of prayer?

2. Do you have the gift of prophecy? If so, how do you know? If not, would you like to receive this gift?

3. In general, to prophesy is to say what God says. Do you recognize the voice of God speaking to you about specific situations? Are you ready to turn His words into a command as you pray about your circumstances?

4. Are you aware of the upcoming times and seasons as you pray? If so, are you ready to speak those out as you pray?

# 8

# Fasting Is a Game Changer

Prayer minister and evangelist Lou Engle came to our church in 2008 as part of his statewide summons for an event known as TheCall, an all-day event attended by thousands and presented as a solemn assembly of prayer in various locations. During his visit, Lou charged us not only to have prayer meetings but also to develop a culture of prayer. He then shared a personal story about fasting—specifically, how the Lord had impressed upon him to go on a forty-day fast.

Lou confessed he did not do the fast at first because he was afraid he would die. Then he received a prophetic word through a prophetic friend. The message was clear: "If you fast for forty days, you won't die." With that, Lou obeyed the Lord and went on an extended fast, only ingesting liquids—and he lived to tell about it.

Lou's story can be inspiring and intimidating all at the same time. I might love the idea of going on a forty-day fast, but I believe I would die, too. I laughed out loud, then, when the

Holy Spirit spoke to my heart, asking me to write a chapter in this book about fasting.

I struggle with fasting. It is not a discipline or theological issue for me. I just happen to be one of those kind, loving individuals who turns into a monster if they do not eat regularly. Hopefully, you hear my humor in that statement, but to a certain extent it is true. People with sensitive physiology and low-blood-sugar problems can take on a certain form of crazy when they have not eaten on time.

Even so, despite this reality, I fast on a regular basis. I just do not fast nearly as long as others, or I do partial fasts. (I will explain this concept later in the chapter.) But stories like the one Lou told used to challenge my confidence.

That is, until I understood the heart of God concerning this discipline.

In the Bible, we find a story about a widow who dropped her last two pennies into the offering box. She did this in front of the wealthier givers and was observed by Jesus in doing so. In response, Jesus called His disciples to Him and said, "Truly I tell you, this poor widow has put more into the treasury than all the others. They all gave out of their wealth; but she, out of her poverty, put in everything—all she had to live on" (Mark 12:43–44).

If you struggle with fasting, too, I want to assure you that Jesus sees the little you do and counts it as being a lot. We do what we can do instead of what we cannot do. Our confidence then rests in knowing the heart of Jesus toward us, rather than in comparing ourselves to others.

## We Are Meant to Fast

When Jesus introduced the Lord's Prayer to His disciples, He began by saying, "When you pray . . ." (Matthew 6:6). Notice that prayer is not an *if* but a *when* matter. The same is true of fasting, as Jesus said in that same teaching, "When you fast . . ." (verse 16).

Jesus taught prayer with fasting, and this was a regular practice of the early Church. It ought to be the same for us.

Accordingly, our church enters each year with either a 21-day or a 40-day fast. We encourage congregants to fast from food as God leads them to do so. Some fast one or two days each week. Some fast a meal each day. Others fast the entire time.

Our church also gathers to pray during that time for specific ministry targets for the next year. In addition, individuals are encouraged to pray for their personal goals and needs.

We have discovered that fasting contains a real turnaround element. It changes circumstances in our favor. For instance:

1. Nathan and Elaina moved into his parents' home in order to save money to buy a house. After a few months, some large expenses came up that made it difficult for them to save money. They fasted and prayed and felt led to give a special offering to the church, in faith for a miracle. Soon after, a woman in the church offered to rent them her home at an affordable price. Later, that same woman sold them her home for a below-market price. Nathan and Elaina became blessed home owners at just 25 years of age.

2. Michelle is the only saved person in her family. She did a partial fast for 21 days and then a water fast for seven more days while praying for the salvation of her mother. When she made a surprise visit to her hometown for her mother's birthday, Michelle asked her mom to receive Jesus into her heart. Her mother said yes and has faithfully attended and served her church ever since.

3. Sean and Kate fasted and prayed for their children to get better jobs and to find affordable housing. Both children had experienced a mix of delays and setbacks, and things were not opening up or working out. After the time of fasting and prayer, both children received new and better jobs and new housing that accommodated their specific needs.

4. Roslyn needed a roommate and a weekend job to make her budget. She felt like she was hitting wall after wall, trying to bridge the gap in her finances. She fasted and prayed, and the Lord dropped a key to obedience in her heart. He told her to give to Him first and trust Him for the rest. As soon as she did that, she found the perfect roommate and was given three weekend jobs to choose from.

The truth is, fasting is a game changer when it comes to unanswered prayer. Add fasting to your prayers, and your answers will come speedily (see Isaiah 58:6–9, especially verse 8). Fasting purifies our bodies, yes, but it also purifies our hearts. It empties us of unbelief and aligns our faith in such a way that we gain triumph over our enemies. We are expected to fast! Fasting is a *when*, not an *if*, matter.

## We Can Fast Three Ways

In the Bible, we see three types of fasts: the absolute fast, the normal fast and the partial fast.

An absolute fast is a fast of abstaining from food and water. Since the body cannot sustain itself without water for more than three days, these fasts are very short. Queen Esther called this kind of fast when her people, the Jews, were being threatened with death (see Esther 4:16). When her people sought God through fasting, they gained a complete turnaround against their enemies. I know of no person who has fasted in this manner myself, although I have read a few stories of those who have tried.

A normal fast is one of abstaining from food but not liquids for a certain number of days. The apostle Paul fasted once for three days and another time for fourteen days (see Acts 9:9; 27:33). Moses and Elijah fasted for forty days (see Exodus 34:28; 1 Kings 19:8). The valiant men of Jabesh Gilead fasted for seven days (see 1 Samuel 31:13). There is no formula for how many days you should fast for a normal fast; it depends on your circumstances. I know many people who have participated in normal fasts for varying lengths of time. They have encountered God in very deep ways through this kind of fast and have experienced turnarounds in difficult circumstances because of it.

Finally, there is the partial fast. This is a fast that allows the consumption of food and liquids but is restricted in some way. In the beginning of Israel's captivity to King Nebuchadnezzar, for example, Daniel and his three friends resolved not to defile themselves with the king's rich foods. They proved this to the guard by eating just vegetables and water for ten days with positive results (see Daniel 1:8–16). Later, Daniel submitted to a 21-day fast in order to seek God concerning the release of His people from captivity (see Daniel 10:2–3). He fasted in similar fashion, with no choice foods, wine or meat for 21 days, and he received a heavenly revelation as a result.

I most often participate in partial fasts, as they are something I can sustain for longer periods of time. My husband, however, prefers a normal fast to a partial fast, saying that, for him, eating too little is harder than not eating at all.

Fasting is an exchange. We exchange food for the Word, for worship and for prayer. It is always done in combination with prayer; otherwise, it is just a diet. Rather, we crucify our flesh and appetite to teach our bodies what to be hungry for. As Jesus said, "Blessed are those who hunger and thirst for righteousness, for they will be filled" (Matthew 5:6). Those who are hungry for God will be filled with Him.

## We Receive a Reward

When we fast, we are not fasting to be seen and admired by people for being spiritual. If we are fasting for those reasons, the Bible says that is all the reward we are going to get (see Matthew 6:16). Rather, when we fast, we are fasting to be seen by God. Therefore, we do not behave in a way that makes it obvious to others that we are fasting.

There is a promise to this kind of fasting. In the words of Jesus, "And your Father, who sees what is done in secret, will reward you" (Matthew 6:18). God rewards what we do in secret. Do you see a person who is marked by God? That person was marked in the secret place.

It reminds me of the experience of our church prayer director, Caroline, who was involved in a serious car accident. While heading to a young adult meeting, she drove onto the freeway, only to enter behind a transport truck that slowed down too quickly. To avoid a collision, she overcorrected, causing her car to spin out of control and roll over twice.

"There were sirens coming from every direction, so I knew it was serious," she said.

Caroline did not break any bones, but her car was totaled. The aftermath of the trauma, however, was intense. She had flashbacks, headaches and migraines. She was easily irritated and felt like she was losing her mind. During our church's annual fast, she joined us and prayed for the church's concerns, including just one personal request for herself: that God would take away all the symptoms that were still with her from the crash.

Within two weeks of fasting, Caroline noticed all of her symptoms had disappeared and she was finally free. Isn't that wonderful? She would have been justified to skip our church's fast completely, given her symptoms. Instead, she chose to fast, making her request known in the secret place, and God rewarded her out in the open.

So, yes, there is a reward to fasting. And the reward, in my mind, is connected to the notion of humility. When we fast, we not only humble ourselves, but also make ourselves weak on purpose—something God rewards with exaltation. So many passages of Scripture speak of the way God exalts the humble (see Matthew 23:12; James 4:10; 1 Peter 5:6).

Believe it or not, we learn humility from God. We were so low in our sin that we could not reach God. God was so high in His righteousness that to reach us, He would have to lower Himself into our messy world to do it. And through the womb of a virgin, He did just that. Jesus entered into our world. He lowered Himself all the way to our level so He could reach us and then save us. As Paul wrote of Jesus, "And being found in appearance as a man, he humbled himself by becoming obedient to death—even death on a cross!" (Philippians 2:8).

But that is not the end of the story. As Jesus humbled Himself all the way to the cross, the Bible says His Father responded to Him lavishly: "Therefore God exalted him to the highest place and gave him the name that is above every name" (verse 9). It is the same principle at work I was just describing, that when we humble ourselves, God will lift us up.

We ought never be afraid to humble ourselves, because on the other end of humility is a reward. Fasting is one such form of humility.

## We Receive a Breakthrough

Throughout its eighty-year history, our church had purchased and built on various properties, and we were blessed as new pastors to find ourselves in a ministry that was property rich, knowing many ministries cannot purchase or even find property.

Unfortunately, the buildings had not been touched in more than fifty years. Paint was cracking and peeling off the exterior, the interiors were musty and dark, and many infrastructure and safety upgrades were needed. My husband presented a challenge to update the main building, and the congregants stepped up with a fierce determination. Deep personal and financial sacrifices were made across the board to transform the facility. In the end, we had a revitalized, modern building and a deeply encouraged congregation.

As soon as the remodeling was complete, Ron began talking about acquiring a second campus. He sat down with a previous pastor of the church, Robert Carrington, and shared his vision. To Ron's surprise, Pastor Carrington had attempted to acquire a second campus forty years before us. He did not succeed, however, because of the same political and spiritual issues we had faced inside the church as new pastors.

We knew acquiring a second campus was going to be next to impossible. We even went into escrow on a piece of land in town but had to give it up because of the economic crash of 2007–2008. So we put the matter to fasting and prayer.

In 2011, during our annual forty days of prayer and fasting, I began having terrible nightmares of death that made modern-day horror films look like child's play. I would wake up with a clear sense of death around me, and it would not lift.

I contacted my lead intercessors for help.

One night, I woke up again with a strong feeling of death and began feeling desperate. I decided to go to our church's prayer chapel and stay there until I was free of it.

As I prayed, the Lord spoke clearly to my heart, saying, *This battle is about life.*

It was a powerful word to my heart. I messaged Ron and shared what the Lord had spoken to me. As I was texting, he was emailing me a message he had received from one of our intercessors. The intercessor had emailed him the details of a dream she had the night before.

"I saw all the dead bodies," she wrote. "You and Jen were arranging them in such a way that the life of God was being poured into their mouths. They were resurrecting!"

What a timely confirmation of the word I had received from the Lord about this being a battle for life.

That same year, we were miraculously given a second church campus. It was a five-acre parcel of land with a church sanctuary, a sports field and a gymnasium that belonged to a Church of Christ church whose ministry had died. The pastor decided we were the church that should have it. We received the campus, remodeled it in nine months with cash and then turned it into a place of life and healing. This forty-year dream that covered two generations was now being realized—and it was a breakthrough that came through prayer and fasting.

When we are not strong enough to break a spiritual barrier through normal means, we need to add fasting to our prayers. When the disciples could not deliver a young boy with a demonic spirit, Jesus rebuked them for their lack of faith, explaining, "This kind can come out by nothing but prayer and fasting"

(Mark 9:29 NKJV). When you have a "this kind" in your life, it is time to pray and get weak through fasting. Mike Bickle, of the International House of Prayer in Kansas City, Missouri, calls fasting *voluntary weakness*. Through fasting, we sow into weakness with our physical bodies and then reap in power (see Isaiah 40:29; 1 Corinthians 15:43).

Pastor Sunday Adelaja from Ukraine has experienced this. He led his people to fast and pray up to three weeks at a time because they needed the power of God to overcome persecution they faced from their government. As a result of their fasting and prayers, the Ukraine government gave them land to build a church[1]—something unheard of in their country.

Recognize that it is one thing to fast for a personal breakthrough, but another thing to fast for a corporate breakthrough. A corporate breakthrough is one that is needed by many people at one time. For example, the Israelites needed a corporate breakthrough from the bondage of Egypt. Today, whole cities, regions and nations need a corporate breakthrough from different kinds of demonic enslavement.

To achieve a corporate breakthrough, a God-fearing leader must call and gather the people to fast and pray. For example, when King Jehoshaphat heard a large army was coming against him, he did not move out in his own strength. He called the people to humble themselves through fasting and praying until they heard the word of the Lord. Then the Lord spoke through Jahaziel, saying, "Do not be afraid or discouraged because of this vast army. For the battle is not yours, but God's" (2 Chronicles 20:15). If you are a pastor or God-fearing leader, one of your responsibilities will be to spearhead corporate breakthrough by gathering the people to fast and pray. When God's people humble themselves and pray, He makes a clear promise to heal their land (see 2 Chronicles 7:14).

## We Receive Our Ministry and Anointing

The Parable of the Talents in Matthew 25 reveals the heart of God to give us more. However, our ability to increase in the things of God is in direct proportion to our ability to carry an anointing from God. King David was anointed three times, and he increased in leadership each time before he entered into his full assignment as the king of Israel.

We find something similar in the example of Jesus. Acts 10:38 tells us, "God anointed Jesus of Nazareth with the Holy Spirit and power, and . . . he went around doing good and healing all who were under the power of the devil, because God was with him." Jesus was anointed with the Holy Spirit and with power. To be *anointed* literally means to be smeared with the Holy Spirit and to be given a gift of power to accomplish a specific task.

Jesus received the Holy Spirit when He was baptized by John the Baptist. His ministry of power, however, was not birthed until after a time of fasting. After Jesus had fasted forty days in the wilderness, He then entered the synagogue and announced to the attendees what He was anointed to do. He quoted Isaiah 61, saying:

> "The Spirit of the Lord is on me, because he has anointed Me to proclaim good news to the poor. He has sent me to proclaim freedom for the prisoners and recovery of sight for the blind, to set the oppressed free, to proclaim the year of the Lord's favor."
>
> Luke 4:18–19

Jesus then began His ministry of power, casting out demons and healing people of diseases.

The anointing was not just reserved for Jesus. It is also reserved for us who believe in His name. Jesus said we would do greater works than He did (see John 14:12). He also said the servant is not above his master (see Matthew 10:24). But we can do greater works than Jesus only to the measure that we have been anointed by the same Holy Spirit.

This anointing is weighty. When the anointing for ministry comes to rest upon you, you may feel it rest like a weighted garment upon your person. The Bible references this as an "ever-increasing glory" (2 Corinthians 3:18) and "eternal glory that far outweighs them all" (2 Corinthians 4:17).

This weighty anointing rests upon our flesh. Since the Bible describes the Spirit being at war with our flesh and our flesh being at war with the Spirit (see Galatians 5:17), this means that in order to sustain the anointing on our flesh, we have to put our flesh down through fasting and prayer. Through fasting, we present our bodies to Jesus as living sacrifices and prepare our flesh to be made into new wineskins, capable of receiving the outpouring of the Spirit (see Romans 12:1; Mark 2:22).

In the New Testament, we see this pattern over and over again—how an anointing for ministry was released after people spent time in prayer and fasting. The apostle Paul was fasting when God called him into his life assignment (see Acts 9:7–9). Paul and Barnabas were called to a specific ministry while they were worshiping and fasting (see Acts 13:2). Jesus, too, went on a fast before His release into full ministry (see Luke 4:1–21). Even as it concerns the coming of the Holy Spirit in Acts 2, the prophet Joel had prophesied the outpouring would come in connection to a fast (see Joel 2:12). Moving forward in history, Jonathan Edwards brought revival to the American colonies before the American Revolution, and this revival outpouring came on the heels of a three-day absolute fast that caused him to vomit and gag violently.[2]

Fasting and prayer is that which prepares our hearts to carry more of what we were made for. The Kingdom of God is always increasing (see Isaiah 9:7). That means we, too, should always be increasing. We do this through the power of fasting and prayer.

## We Can Fast Successfully

Fasting is a spiritual discipline that brings heavenly rewards. It is also a physical discipline. To fast successfully, it is important to know how to enter into and exit a fast in ways that heal your body without damaging it.

Let me tell you a story that is the opposite of a successful fast. Nearly one hundred years ago, a family gave their personal finances to purchase land for a new work in Turlock, California. The late evangelist Aimee Semple McPherson had introduced the city to the Holy Spirit, and a Spirit-filled community had emerged that needed property.

This same family's grandson, Bill Larson, became an established citywide evangelist, with discipleship studies happening in his home nearly every night. Thousands of people were converted as a result. Bill was so zealous that he finally quit his job, choosing to trust the Lord for his provision. He wanted to reach every unsaved person he could.

This man was responsible for the conversion and discipleship of my husband, Ron, as a teenager. He found Ron smoking in a local park and led him to Christ. Bill then invited Ron to a Bible study and discipled him there. A decade later, my husband was named the senior pastor of Harvest Christian Center in Turlock, California, which we discovered later was the original property purchased by Bill's grandparents.

Bill died at age 62 in 2015, but his legacy continues.

Do you want to know Bill's cause of death? It is hard to believe, but he died from too much fasting. Bill fasted often, but this time he had gone past the biblical limit of forty days, and it killed him.

In our zeal for breakthrough and anointing, we need to recognize our limitations and know how to fast successfully. This is a discipline that impacts us spirit, soul and body and therefore requires thought and preparation.

Here are some guidelines to help prepare you for a successful fast.

## 1. Commit to Fasting

Fasting is never convenient and hardly something we feel like doing. But we cannot base our fasting on our feelings. Instead, we are to purpose our hearts to seek the Lord with fasting as an act of our will and out of obedience to Jesus' instruction. Remember He said, "When you fast . . ." (Matthew 6:16), assuming it would happen.

## 2. Assess Your Reasons

When we pray, we worship the Lord but also seek His hand of provision. The same goes for fasting. We have already covered that God openly rewards what we do in secret. Therefore, we need to approach fasting in the knowledge of the rewards we seek. Be purposeful while fasting.

## 3. List the Promises

In Isaiah 58, we see that the people of God were frustrated. They were fasting and praying, but God was not responding. The reason? They were fasting in a spirit of strife and competition, and they were doing it with selfish motives. To keep ourselves from the same mistake, we will want to write down the verses that support what we are seeking in our fast. Taking this extra step forces us to evaluate our hearts and to prove things out through the Word.

## 4. Prepare Your Body

If you are preparing to go on an extended fast, begin limiting your food intake prior to your fast. If you gorge yourself ahead of time, your body has a more difficult time entering a normal fast.

Limit your intake of caffeine (unless you want to experience a terrific headache at the onset!). During an extended fast, many people ingest juices and broths to sustain their energy. Be sure to drink plenty of purified water, up to a gallon a day, to flush your system and eliminate poisons from your body. Signs of physical detoxification vary from person to person but typically include headaches, acne and bad breath, which pass in a few days.

After you end your fast, you should exit it the same way you entered it. I made the mistake twice to end a five-day fast with a loaded roast-beef sandwich from a nearby restaurant. I completely lost my brain with hunger, and both times I was sick to my stomach for over a week. My husband, on the other hand, takes a few days to a week to exit an extended fast, choosing light broths and soups, then vegetables, then dairy and meats last.

## 5. Declare Your Fast

We see in the Bible that people like Jehoshaphat, Ezra, Jeremiah and the Ninevites proclaimed their fasts and the reasons for them before the Lord. This means we do not declare our fasts within the quiet recesses of our hearts. Instead, we verbalize them out loud before the Lord, telling Him that we are fasting for a particular time frame and why we are doing it. Remember, "By your words you will be justified" (Matthew

12:37 NKJV). The declaration makes our fasting official in the courts of heaven and brings it under the covering of the Lord.

## 6. Pick a Friend

My best seasons of fasting have happened when I fasted with our church. I believe this is because there is more synergy, encouragement and accountability in the company of others who are doing it, too. It seems we are more successful this way. For that reason, I recommend that you conduct your personal fasts with a friend or two. That way, when one of you starts to fail at it, the other can pray and offer encouragement. Remember, "Two are better than one. . . . If either of them falls down, one can help the other up" (Ecclesiastes 4:9–10).

## 7. Recognize Opposing Forces

Jesus was led by the Holy Spirit to fast for forty days in the wilderness and was tempted by Satan throughout (see Matthew 4:1–11). We can learn from His experience how to guard ourselves when we fast.

Satan first attacked Jesus' identity, saying, "If you are the Son of God . . ." (verse 3). When you fast, remember who you are in Christ. If you are attacked in your identity, do what Jesus did. He refuted the attack by quoting Scriptures in their proper context, thus reaffirming His identity.

Next, Satan took Jesus to the highest point of the temple, trying to trick Him into committing suicide. He said, "If you are the Son of God, throw yourself down" (verse 6). I have never felt suicidal during a fast, but I often experience high emotionalism or extreme thinking. Things I thought I forgave might come to the surface, or I will take something personally that normally would not bother me. This is a time to be self-aware and to have a plan to help you get through this kind of weakness if you are susceptible.

Finally, Satan tried to attack Jesus' relationship with God, saying, "Bow down and worship me" (verse 9). This attack from Satan during a fast usually shows up as despair, discouragement or feelings of distance from God. Again we learn from Jesus that our relationship with God is based not on feelings but on the written Word, as Jesus quoted Scripture back to the devil each and every time.

There are great rewards to fasting—spiritual, emotional and physical rewards. Through fasting, we subdue the voice of our flesh and increase our spiritual sensitivity. We hear the voice of God better and begin to discern the spirit realm more accurately. Discerning the spirit realm allows us to pray more effectively because we can pray more intelligently. For us to discern well, the Holy Spirit releases a powerful gift, called the discerning of spirits. Let us turn to that gift next in our study of intercessory prayer.

## Kingdom Prayer Principles

1. Biblical fasting is refraining from food for a spiritual purpose.
2. Fasting purifies not only our bodies, but also our hearts. It empties us of unbelief and aligns our faith in a way that allows us to triumph over our enemies.
3. Jesus says about fasting, "When you fast . . ." (Matthew 6:16). Notice fasting is not an *if* but a *when* matter. We are expected to fast.
4. Fasting is an exchange. We exchange food for the Word, worship and prayer. Fasting teaches us to hunger after God.

131

5. When we humble ourselves, God will lift us up. One way we humble ourselves is through fasting.

6. When we are not strong enough to break through a barrier, we need to add fasting to our prayers. God meets us at our point of weakness and gives us His strength to break through.

7. In the New Testament, we see the same pattern over and over again: The anointing for ministry is released after people pray and fast.

## Thoughts for Reflection

1. Do you fast? If so, how often and how much?

2. What role does comparison play in your fasting experiences? Why might comparison be a poor motivation to fast?

3. How have you experienced a turnaround in difficult circumstances as a result of a fast?

4. How is your sensitivity to the voice of God impacted when you fast?

5. How has the anointing on your life for ministry been impacted by your fasting?

# 9

# How to Pray Intelligently

In August 2013, I issued an urgent invitation to my social media network to attend one of our weekly prayer services. Our state had just passed outlandish transgender legislation that targeted our public school system. It was so loosely written that the law posed serious safety and privacy issues for our schoolkids, regardless of their perceived sexual orientation. We needed to pray as a community and seek the Lord on what to do.

As people walked into our prayer chapel, I welcomed almost each one with a hug. I knew most of them, but there were a few I did not recognize. I felt unsettled about one woman in particular, but I did not know why. I had seen her at one of our church conferences before. Other than that, I did not know who she was or where she was from.

I greeted her and asked her a few casual questions to try to locate her spirit. As she talked, I could identify the issue: She was not submitted to authority.

Nothing the woman said or did gave me that insight. I knew it by the Holy Spirit.

I left the room as the attendees worshiped together, praying to myself and thinking I should call a pastor I knew in another town to ask him about it.

When I called him up, all I said on the phone was, "Do you know this woman?"

He could not contain his reaction. He said, "That woman is the most underhanded, rebellious and divisive person I've encountered in years!"

It was everything I suspected, but I needed to hear a confirmation.

The next day, a different pastor from another city surprised me with a phone call. He was calling to warn me about the same woman.

That was the last time I saw her.

How did I know, without any evidence, that the woman was going to be a problem? I knew it by the gift of discerning of spirits. This gift comes from the Holy Spirit and enables you to distinguish between spirits that are divine, demonic or human. It also provides you with a supernatural ability to discern the hidden motives of the heart, both good and bad.

Now, this is not the same thing as turning an evil eye toward others or being suspicious, which are heart issues. It is a divine ability given by God that allows you to see past the surface and know the spirit and heart motives behind people and situations.

This gift is mentioned by name in 1 Corinthians 12:10, alongside several other supernatural gifts. It is a gift that works in tandem with intercession, enabling us to be alert to the specific schemes of the enemy as we faithfully watch and pray, and that is why you need to know about it.

## Watch and Pray

During His final hours of freedom, Jesus led his disciples to the Garden of Gethsemane. He said, "Stay here and keep watch with me" (Matthew 26:38).

What was He watching for?

He was watching and waiting in prayer for His enemy to come—only He was not going to be delivered. He was going to the cross.

However, instead of watching and praying with Him, the disciples kept falling asleep. When He found them sleeping, He warned them, "Watch and pray so that you will not fall into temptation" (verse 41). Then He left them twice more to pray on His own, only to return and find them sleeping again. When His enemy came to betray Him moments later, the disciples succumbed to the situation and deserted Him. Not one stood by His side.

An intercessor not only prays for God's Kingdom to come, but also watches and prays to keep the enemy out. We watch and pray to keep the enemy out of our lives, the lives of our family members, our churches, our cities and more.

The apostle Peter warns us, "Be alert and of sober mind. Your enemy the devil prowls around like a roaring lion looking for someone to devour" (1 Peter 5:8). Satan is looking for an opportunity to attack, but God is looking to reveal it before it happens. However, He can reveal the plans of the enemy only to those who are alert and remain ready. If we are not paying attention in prayer—if we are spiritually asleep—we will miss God's divine warnings, and Satan will come in to devour whatever he wants.

Think about it like this. In my home, we have an alarm system and two very alert dogs that help us feel protected. Occasionally, my dogs will go on barking marathons at night, probably to entertain the rest of the dogs in the neighborhood. I sleep right through those bark fests, giving them as little attention as possible.

Our security alarm also activates itself in the middle of the night from time to time, which is impossible to sleep through. I think it is possessed, but my husband says it is the batteries or a power outage. I am not sure why, but I never think we are experiencing a break-in when the alarm begins to sound. All I care about is finding the keypad in the dark just to shut the noisy thing off. I never check the house, I never look around, and I always go right back to sleep. I am thankful Ron has a different attitude! He will check around the house and even go outside, fully ready to take out the bad guys if needed.

Ron carries the heart of a watchman for our home. He guards and protects it, responding to any alarms, no matter what time of night. In the Bible, a watchman was a protector who watched over crops, city gates or walls (see Isaiah 62:6; Jeremiah 51:12; Ezekiel 33:2–3). When an enemy approached, the watchman alerted the people by sounding an alarm.

In the same way, God is sounding spiritual alarms to His watchmen and watchwomen. He is saying, *Wake up. Be alert. Take out the bad guys trying to break in!*

Adam, the original watchman, failed his assignment. God placed him in the Garden of Eden to "tend and keep it" (Genesis 2:15 NKJV). This word *keep* in Hebrew is the word *shamar*, which means "to keep, watch and preserve." The word has a protective element to it. When the serpent came, Adam did not raise the alarm. He did not protect the garden. Instead, he let Satan—the ultimate bad guy—come in, and Satan devoured all.

When we see destruction and evil in our society and in the nations, this is the handiwork of Satan gone unchecked. He is the thief who comes to steal, kill and destroy, and somehow he has been let in (see John 10:10). The evil we see also speaks of the need for more spiritual watchmen and watchwomen who will stand guard against the plans of the enemy and boldly declare, "Not on my watch!"

The apostle Paul exhorts us not to be outwitted by Satan and to be aware of his schemes (see 2 Corinthians 2:11). That means we can be deceived or naïve to what he is really doing. Satan operates under the cloak of deception and darkness. As we stand watch in intercession and pray, the Holy Spirit desires to give us His ability to discern the spirit realm so we can pray intelligently.

## Develop a Framework

We also need to know that events are happening in the spiritual realm all the time. We are given many glimpses into this reality in the Bible. For example, consider the story of Job. Job was "the greatest man among all the people of the East" (Job 1:3). He was blameless, upright and feared the Lord. He was wealthy and blessed of God.

And then, in one day, he lost everything. Armies attacked and killed his servants and stole most of his herds. A firestorm and windstorm destroyed what was left, including his children. He became ill, with boils all over his body.

What was happening here? Was he facing such negative circumstances by chance, or was something else going on?

You probably know the story. These were not natural circumstances. Job was in a spiritual battle. Satan was competing for Job's heart, but God was confident Job would stay loyal to Him— which he did, and God gave Job back double for his trouble.

Through this account, we notice the Holy Spirit pulling back the curtain of the spirit realm to provide a framework for discerning present-day circumstances. We need such a framework because the spirit realm is full of intangibles and things that can be difficult to define. The apostle Paul alluded to this when he was caught up to the third heaven, seeing paradise and hearing "inexpressible things" (2 Corinthians 12:4). I, too, have been to heaven—three times total—and it is true. You cannot define or even speak about what is there because it is too glorious to express. We need a framework to help us understand it.

To flow in the gift of discerning of spirits with a proper framework, then, we have to learn from the Word the possibilities of the spirit realm. Job's plight, for starters, was a conflict between Satan and God concerning Job's loyalty (see Job 1:6–12). In the book of Daniel, we find that a demonic prince of Persia once withheld Daniel's answer to prayer (see Daniel 10:1–14). In another instance, an army of angels came to fight for Elisha (see 2 Kings 6:15–17). These examples begin to tell us what is possible in the spirit realm.

In the New Testament, we find more stories to broaden our framework. We see Jesus encounter a man possessed by a legion—thousands—of demons (see Luke 8:26–39), Philip caught away by the Spirit so that he vanished from the place that he was (see Acts 8:26–40) and an angel letting Peter out of prison (see Acts 12:5–11). Again, these provide us with glimpses into the spirit realm and an awareness of the possibilities at work in the situations we face.

Until we have a good framework for what is possible, we will struggle to discern well. We will not grasp what the Holy Spirit is revealing to us. Instead, we will be presumptuous or naïve about what is really happening. We cannot pray effectively out of presumption or naïveté. We have to pray with the right information if we are going to see the right answers.

For instance, not every problem is a demon. Some curses come from God; some come from people. The gift of discerning of spirits will help you know what you are really dealing with.

Here is a case in point, taken from the Old Testament. A famine once took place during the reign of King David, and after the third consecutive year, he asked the Lord about it (see 2 Samuel 21). The Lord told David it was the result of an injustice committed against the Gibeonites by the former King Saul and his army. The Israelites had vowed to protect the Gibeonites, but Saul, in his zeal, tried to destroy them. So David approached the Gibeonites and asked what he could do to atone for the injustice done against them. The Gibeonites requested seven descendants of Saul for the purpose of execution. David delivered the seven men, the Gibeonites executed them, and the famine was broken.

Now, I am not suggesting execution as a means of atoning for curses. I am using this story to show you that different possibilities exist than we might expect. You need to learn how to discern between a curse and a demonic binding.

We faced one such matter of discernment in our own city and were able to overturn it through prayer. The city had a long-standing issue with arson, especially in the downtown area. It had been an issue for as long as I could remember. In the back of my mind, I worried our church building might be torched, as we had seen several buildings go down like that over the years.

By divine accident, I found an old story from the early days of our city about a situation involving the Chinese community.[1] The story described early Turlock as having anti-Chinese sentiments. When tents caught fire in the Chinese community in those early days, a saloonkeeper referred to as "Old Purdy" gave the Chinese settlers buckets of kerosene disguised as water to help put out the fires, which resulted in extreme damage. The story said the Chinese men then began hailing curses from God at Old Purdy and the onlookers.

When I ran across this story, I felt a tug from the Holy Spirit. These tugs feel as if someone is lightly yanking a rope that is attached to you at chest level. That tug was my point of discernment. Through that tug, I knew this curse was still activating the arson events in our city. So at our next prayer service, we said a simple prayer: "Lord, forgive our city's great-grandfathers for persecuting the Chinese community with fire. We bless the Chinese community, and we break the curse of arson off our city."

Since we prayed that prayer, there has not been any recorded arson in our downtown city area.

Like most gifts of the Holy Spirit, the gift of discerning of spirits is multifaceted and functions in different ways, depending on its context. If you are a leader, for example, you may discern various anointings on people's lives and begin to place them in your church or organization appropriately. If you are a grade-level teacher or children's worker, you may be able to discern the victories and struggles in your children without being told what they are. If you are a police officer, you may discern the spirits at work in neighborhoods and the places you patrol.

In the context of intercession, the gift of discernment of spirits provides you with spiritual intelligence so you can pray with precision.

## Use Your Senses

The gift of discerning of spirits is highly misunderstood in its operation. People think they will discern through their minds. However, you do not discern things with your mind. This is not an ability that allows you to rationalize something through your intellect.

Rather, you discern through your emotions and your senses—through sight, taste, touch, smell and hearing. You experience spiritual information before you have rational evidence for it. It takes a mature spirit: "But solid food is for the mature, who because of practice have their senses trained to discern good and evil" (Hebrews 5:14 NASB).

The Bible shows us a variety of ways this gift can manifest. In Acts 12, for example, Peter is in prison and sleeping between two soldiers the night before his public trial. An angel appears, strikes him on the side and tells him to get up before leading him out of prison. Notice Peter *sees, feels* and *hears* the angel.

Did you know you cannot recognize or identify an angel, as Peter did, unless the gift of discerning of spirits is in operation? Otherwise, you would not be able to distinguish it. Peter did not even think what was happening was real until he was outside the prison and the angel had disappeared (see verses 9 and 11).

Paul experienced the gift of discerning of spirits, too, when he encountered a slave girl in Philippi. He and Silas had traveled to the area based on a dream, and the slave girl met them on their way to prayer. She followed them for several days, shouting, "These men are servants of the Most High God, who are telling you the way to be saved" (Acts 16:17).

Now, I am not saying this was normal behavior, but at best, she could have just been excited. At worst, she could have been behaviorally or mentally challenged. Was the slave girl unable to behave appropriately, or was something else going on?

If you read the story, you find out right away she had a demonic spirit by which she predicted the future. It is not clear, though, if the apostles knew she had such a spirit at the outset. It was several days before Paul dealt with her. But we see

Paul's reaction plainly. It says he became highly annoyed and then cast the spirit out of her (see verse 18). The reason I draw that out—Paul being highly annoyed—is because that kind of annoyance is often a point of discernment.

Here is what I mean. One time, a pastor colleague of mine in New Jersey had a church member who was secretly meeting with other congregants to try to start his own church. On the surface, the man and his wife appeared to be serving well. My pastor friend had no reason to suspect anything was amiss.

The church member had written a book, and a display for his book was in the church lobby when I went to speak at the church one weekend. As I walked by the display, I noticed the joy I had been carrying turned to a sudden and severe annoyance. I wanted to kick the book display over, which would have been crazy. It was so irrational that I wondered, *Am I having some kind of fit or breakdown?*

It all came out soon enough. Several weeks later, the pastor of the church called me to share that one of his church members had left the church with several other families to start a new church. He mentioned the man had written a book that the church had displayed in its lobby to support the man and his message. I remembered my strange reaction to the book display and confirmed it was for the same man's book. My annoyance had been the gift of discerning of spirits in operation.

If you do not know to pay attention, you will miss when the Holy Spirit is speaking to you through your senses. The manifestation of this gift varies from person to person and covers a wide spectrum. For example, one woman I know discerns the presence of the Lord through what smells like baked cookies. Now, the Bible does refer to the fragrance of Christ as a sweet-smelling aroma (see 2 Corinthians 2:15; Philippians 4:18). To this woman, He smells like a Mrs. Fields cookie store!

My husband, Ron, on the other hand, discerns things through a general feeling inside himself. In his words, he just "knows what he knows."

For me, I notice a metallic taste in my mouth. The Holy Spirit has helped me understand this happens when I am near a person who has a spirit of violence on them. I can also "smell" an unclean spirit, "sense" the spirit of fear on my skin and "feel" a religious spirit through a certain kind of headache. For a long time, I did not know these feelings were connected to anything spiritual until I asked the Lord for an explanation.

When you begin to notice things in your senses that have no explanation, recognize it is an invitation for dialogue with the Lord. He is inviting you into a conversation! As you seek Him for clarity, you can turn the positive points of discernment you receive into worship and the negative points you receive into intercession.

The gift of discerning of spirits is primarily sensory, and we learn through trial and error to distinguish what we are sensing and then turn it into prayer. If this is a new gift in your life, it can be helpful and even therapeutic to dialogue with a mature mentor about what you are sensing and what you believe it is connected to. Dutch Sheets wrote in his book *Watchman Prayer*, "Skilled watchmen could sometimes even recognize the runners 'by their stride' before ever seeing their faces."[2] There is a connection between discerning well and maturity, and discerning well comes through practice (see Hebrews 5:14).

## Accept the Gift

Remember that this is a supernatural gift, much like the gift of prophecy or the gift of miracles. It flows in different strengths between different people. There are a surprising number of people who have this gift but do not know it. All too often, they mistake their giftedness for being crazy.

Here is one such story. Linda (not her real name) walked into our prayer service for the first time one night. The prayer team, full of people who are very sensitive, detected her issues. They were able to keep control of the room's atmosphere and continue the service, despite what Linda brought in. She would close her eyes at times or drift into Bible reading. Other times, she would look around the room as if confused. She was swift to leave at the end.

As time went on, various people tried to reach out to her. She would get angry enough to shut them down or argue with them enough to keep them at a distance. I was one of the few people who could reach her, and she finally confessed the problem. She was hearing voices. She wanted my help but did not, in the end, align with what was necessary to bring healing and wholeness to this spiritual sensitivity she had been given.

I understood what Linda was experiencing. I heard voices even as a small child. I connected it to being in tune with the spirit realm. I shared in an earlier chapter that I did not become a Christian until I was a freshman in college and that a year later I was delivered from occult spirits. I was set free and experienced real authority in Christ, only to be thrown into a very loud and intense world of voices. I was hearing voices in the air, voices in my mind and voices of spirits. It was intense, and things never did quiet down.

At first, I wanted to be alone as much as possible. Being in crowds was painful, and I began to crave and treasure silence. When things did not change, it left me with the typical questions: *Am I schizophrenic? Am I demonized? Or do I have an atypical gift from God?*

The reason I thought this might be a gift from God was because I had started to hear people's thoughts. Now, I knew husbands and wives often knew each other's thoughts without thinking too much about it. I knew it to be a sign of intimacy between two people who know each other well. We also read in the Bible that Jesus could perceive people's thoughts and would answer their thoughts appropriately (see Mark 2:8; Luke 6:8). This gave Him an advantage in difficult crowds.

Since I could locate my experience in the Bible, I felt better about it—but not for reasons you might think. I did not know everyone's waking thought, nor did I want to. Rather, I would hear or feel someone's strongest thought and would even attempt to speak into it when I felt God's permission.

Now, years later, this activity flows quite naturally with me, and I usually do not even think about it before I say something revealing to the person I am with. This has often earned me the uncomfortable rebuke, "Get out of my thoughts!"

But it took me years to sort out I had received the gift of discerning of spirits. I did not know it for a long time.

Because everything has a voice to it, through this gift, I was hearing or feeling the voice of pretty much everything until I learned how to manage it. I will try to describe how this works. God created everything with His word, and all creation is designed to praise Him. If the people of earth fail to praise God, the Bible says even the rocks will cry out (see Luke 19:40). I am mentioning this to demonstrate that everything has the capacity to "sound off" under certain conditions. The gift of discerning of spirits will cause you to sense the nature of the sound for the purpose of intercession.

Now, there is a voice (or "sound") on land, in the air, in people groups, in animals, in objects, and on and on. That sound can become painful or aggravating when something has corrupted it. I might hear or feel the voice of the problem in my mind or on my skin or in my emotions, just to name a few possibilities.

For example, the day before the 9/11 attacks, I had a terrible feeling of foreboding that I could not explain. When you do not know what it is, your mind can try to compensate with explanations that are not accurate. My first inaccurate thought was that my house was on fire. My second inaccurate thought was that there was going to be a violent rift at a meeting I was scheduled to attend that evening. Neither thought was accurate or even logical, but I sensed fire and then violence, and then my mind tried to piece it together. I spent the afternoon praying in my prayer language because I was unable to get a grip on my feelings. The next morning, when the news of the terror attacks came out, I understood what was behind the things I was discerning.

Although I manage it much better now, I still walk in this level of intensity almost daily. This gift has taken me into the place of intercession unlike anything else. I have also counseled too many people to count who have the same gift, which is why I wanted to touch on it in this book. If you have the gift of discerning of spirits in this much strength, you can see how it could be mistaken for schizophrenia or bipolar disorder. If that is you, will you consider that you are not crazy but actually have a gift?

Kris Vallotton once said, "If you don't manage your discernment, it will manage you." We manage the strength of this gift through a heavy diet of the Word and prayer and by living a sanctified life. We direct it toward intercession until our peace returns to us. When our peace has returned to us, then we know we have established God's Kingdom effectively through prayer (see Isaiah 9:7).

The gift of discerning of spirits allows us to watch and pray intelligently. As James says, "The prayer of a righteous person is powerful and effective" (James 5:16). We are supposed to be effective in prayer, not ineffective. This gift, in all its unusual manifestations, sharpens our intercession.

## Kingdom Prayer Principles

1. The gift of discerning of spirits comes from the Holy Spirit and enables us to distinguish between spirits—divine, demonic and human. It is also a supernatural ability to discern the hidden motives of the heart.

2. This gift is not the same as having an evil eye toward others or being suspicious, which are heart issues.

3. The gift of discerning of spirits works in tandem with intercession, enabling us to be alert to the specific schemes of the enemy as we watch and pray.

4. We have to develop, from the Word, a framework of possibilities in the spirit realm if we are going to discern well. Otherwise, we will not be able to grasp what the Holy Spirit is revealing to us.

5. This gift is primarily sensory, and we discern the spirit realm through our emotions and our five physical senses, not through our intellects.

6. When we begin to notice things happening in our senses that have no explanation, we must recognize it as an invitation for dialogue with the Lord. The positive points of discernment become worship; the negative points become intercession.

7. There are a surprising number of people who have the gift of discerning of spirits and do not know it. All too often, they mistake their giftedness for being crazy.

## Thoughts for Reflection

1. In what ways have you been able to recognize the presence of God through your senses? The presence of evil?

2. Do you often second-guess or feel bad about yourself when you discern evil in a person or a situation? What is a more constructive way to process this information?

3. Do you find yourself sensitive to nearly everything? Do you struggle with noise and crowds, finding it difficult to think and process unless you are fully alone? Do you dislike that about yourself, and have you considered that you might have a strong expression of this gift?

4. Do the possibilities of the spirit realm draw you into dialogue with God and intercession? Or do they shut you down with fear? What is the Holy Spirit saying about that?

# 10

# We Are a House of Prayer

All over the earth, we see a movement of prayer taking place. Paul's simple admonition to the Thessalonians to "pray continually" (1 Thessalonians 5:17) has resulted in a surge of 24/7 prayer gatherings around the globe that attract old and young alike. These gatherings can be found in Canada, Germany, Switzerland, Spain, South America, Africa, China, America—the list goes on.

Kim Catherine Marie Kollins, a nun from Texas who led a 24/7 prayer ministry among one hundred million renewed Catholics, once said:

> Everywhere I turn I seem to hear this same call to prayer being proclaimed—prayer for cities, prayer for nations. Everywhere I look I see writings calling the people of God to intense worship and adoration and intercession. Many new prayer initiatives are being called forth—houses of prayer are springing up, prayer mountains and prayer vigils are being held in response to this prompting of the Holy Spirit.[1]

The practice of day-and-night prayer has its foundations in the Old Testament, beginning with King David. On his inauguration day as king of Israel, David commanded the Ark of the Covenant be carried by the Levitical priests into the new capital of Jerusalem. It was received with a loud celebration of songs and with dancing and then was placed inside the Tabernacle. David appointed hundreds of singers and musicians to worship, to give thanks and to petition the Lord day and night, something that had never been done before (see 1 Chronicles 15–16).

We see this pattern of day-and-night prayer continuing with David's son Solomon, but now the new Temple replaced the less-permanent Tabernacle. Leaders of Judah and Israel that came later, such as Jehoshapat, Joash, Hezekiah, Josiah, Ezra and Nehemiah, were also conscientious to reestablish day-and-night prayer, appointing singers and musicians to their places "according to the commands of David and his son Solomon" (Nehemiah 12:45).

By the time Jesus came to earth, the Temple's night-and-day prayer expression had been replaced with religious politics and disreputable commerce. Provoked by this, Jesus arrived at the Temple with whips in hand and began driving out the buyers and sellers and the animals for sale before turning over by force the tables of the money changers (see John 2:13–16). He then rebuked the Temple crowd with a prophecy from Isaiah, saying, "It is written, 'My house will be called a house of prayer'" (Matthew 21:13; cf. Isaiah 56:7).

The prophet Isaiah had seen eight hundred years into the future—to this very moment at the Temple—and called forth the priorities that needed to be in place. It was to be "a house of prayer for all nations" (Isaiah 56:7). This makes prayer the first ministry of the Church. And the reach of our prayers is meant to be the nations.

I believe this is why the Church was birthed in the Upper Room during a prayer meeting. This is why the first outreach flowed from that place of prayer to the visiting nations in Jerusalem, resulting in three thousand conversions to Christ (see Acts 2). The Holy Spirit was communicating through this that prayer is the first thing we do and that, as a result, the nations turn to Christ.

We also see the early Church being unceasing in prayer. We read how "they devoted themselves . . . to prayer" (Acts 2:42). They prayed as individuals and together. Again, the apostle Paul exhorted the early Church to "pray continually" (1 Thessalonians 5:17). They were fervent in prayer and prayed in their homes, at the Temple and in the streets (see James 5:16; Acts 3:1–2). Over and over, these activities are demonstrated in the Scriptures to encourage us to make prayer the first thing we do everywhere.

The praying Church overturns demonic plans, puts angels on assignment, cleanses atmospheres and creates conditions for the visible invasion of the Word of God into the nations. As spiritual kings and priests on the earth, it is our honor and privilege to govern our whole world through prayer.

## Praying for Nations

It is hard to believe that prior to the Prohibition movement in the early 1900s, America had developed a severe problem with alcohol that dated back to the Puritans. Families were ravaged by it. Work productivity was affected by it. It was all too common for workers not to come in on Mondays because of their weekend hangovers. As Daniel Okrent, historian and author of *Last Call: The Rise and Fall of Prohibition*, puts it, "America had been awash in drink almost from the start—wading hip-deep in it, swimming in it, at various times its history nearly drowning in it."[2] Abraham Lincoln referred to the problem as "the devastator,"[3] saying alcohol "commonly entered into the first draught of an infant, and the last draught of the dying man."[4]

In December 1873, Eliza Jane Trimble Thompson led 75 women to war in prayer over this monumental social problem. Eliza was a devout Methodist, the daughter of an Ohio governor, the wife of a judge and the mother of eight. She was a quiet woman but was chosen by her peers to take the lead. On a cold winter day that December, this group of women marched out of church and over to the various saloons, hotels and drugstores—not to protest, but to pray. As they reached these establishments, they dropped to their knees in prayer for the souls of the owners of each place.

They prayed for eleven days, up to six hours at a time, until nine of the town's thirteen drinking places closed their doors. Saloon owners began to repent, which set off a storm of similar prayer actions in the Midwest and New England. Not all of the saloon closures were permanent, but this act of prayer was the tipping point for America to begin dealing with its alcohol problem. A more sober America emerged through legislation and industry regulation, undergirded by the fervent prayers of the Church and the fiery preaching of evangelists like Billy Sunday and others like him.

This is what happens when we, the Church, commit ourselves to prayer. Prayer is an exercise of spiritual government. It is our priestly function and the most powerful exercise of godly authority on the earth. It invites the atmosphere of heaven and the will of God into the earth's domain and establishes territorial occupation.

We need to cultivate a culture of prayer and embrace a lifestyle of prayer. To understand this better, consider the prayer culture of Muslims and its impact. Muslims pray five times a day and fast one month each year, during the lunar month of Ramadan. When they fast, it is a total fast—no water or food—from sunup to sunset. In Muslim-dominated areas around the globe, an audible call to prayer is given from the mosques, in response to which persons kneel to pray in the direction of Mecca.

Muslims have a culture of prayer, and it is part of their lifestyle. They also have what I call a "governmental" mindset, meaning an intention to infiltrate every aspect of society—culture, politics, economics and more—wherever they live, including America. By way of example, we learned through a Michigan church-planter named Chilly Chilton that the city of Hamtramck, located within inner-city Detroit, broadcasts the Islamic "call to prayer" from mosques throughout the city five times a day.[5] How did an American city become so immersed in Islam as to freely broadcast that religion's call to prayer? I believe it happened as a result of their prayer culture, which is a spiritual and governmental act in their eyes and which has enabled them to occupy more territory.

I once was in a closed Muslim nation, ministering to congregants and leaders of an active missions organization and in the underground Church. I was scheduled to speak about prophetic intercession at a conference beginning on a Friday evening. On Friday afternoon, I began to experience spiritual warfare. First, the power went out in my apartment—something that, according to the owner, was not normal. When the power went out, I began to feel a strong disorientation in my mind. This type of disorientation is something I have learned is a symptom of religious witchcraft active in the atmosphere. Just a few moments later, I managed to cut my finger quite badly and could not stop the bleeding. All I could do was wrap my finger tightly in tissue. I dressed clumsily, then went to brush my hair and noticed medium-sized clumps falling out. I have lots of thick hair and began to pray I would not show any bald spots, as the clumps would not stop coming out.

I was growing in righteous rage through that series of incidents, realizing a very real demonic presence was in the atmosphere. I was informed later that the local Muslims meet on Fridays at the mosque to pray. I believe I was bumping into their prayers—that I was in the atmosphere of those prayers. This created all sorts of disturbances I had to navigate in order to get to the meeting that evening.

I share this story to demonstrate that prayer is an exercise of power and government in the spiritual atmosphere and creates tangible and measurable results on earth. Christians who do not pray or do not make an effort to pray as a church community forfeit their authority, not realizing they are the reason many people remain hell-chained in their communities with no other means of deliverance. This is a sobering thought. Come on, Church! It is time to pray, and it is time to pray unceasingly.

God has a big vision for prayer on the earth. He declared His Church to be a house of prayer for all nations, in fact, remember? So, why does God have big vision for prayer? To fulfill His dream. He said His government would only increase and not decrease (see Isaiah 9:7). His heart is for entire nations, as well as those who lead them. This includes modern-day Nebuchadnezzars, socialist rulers, religious leaders, dictators and corrupt elected officials. Churches that consistently pray together will change their regions and nations.

Here are a few examples:

1. **China.** I travel to China each year and minister in not-so-typical places. There are strong Christians everywhere you go in China, and they are praying and evangelizing

passionately. According to a 2014 article in *The Telegraph*, China is on course to become the most Christian nation within fifteen years.[6]

2. **Almolonga, Guatemala.** This city was known for its alcoholism, violence and idol worship. Its evangelical churches were small and persecuted. After a violent attempt against his life, pastor Mariano Riscajche began to hold regular prayer services with his small congregation. They began to lay hold of heaven's atmosphere in their city and to proclaim the promises of God to their land. In time, men and women began to get delivered from demons and commit their lives to Jesus Christ. The phenomenon spread as prayer grew and grew, until the city experienced a complete transformation. Now, with 85 percent of the population professing faith in Christ, the city of Almolonga has closed all four of its jails and all but three saloons. The buildings and streets have been renamed after biblical characters. The most notable transformation came in the shape of its miraculously large and prosperous agricultural produce, which received global attention.[7]

3. **Ukraine.** Pastor Sunday Adelaja began with a prayer group in a dilapidated apartment, only to build a vast and powerful church in the capital city of Kiev. Still, his church was persecuted to the point of no longer having a meeting space. The government took every measure possible to contain the church. But at the word of the Lord, Pastor Sunday's congregation challenged their government in open protest. Their protest, fueled by hours of prayer and fasting, resulted in an unprecedented decision by the government to give them more than six acres of land to build upon. Later, the church played a key role in a major presidential election that defied Russian influence

and ushered in a pro-Western president by the name of Viktor Yushchenko.[8]

4. **Panama.** General Manuel Noriega was known to practice voodoo and other forms of magic in consortium with occult leaders. He was highly impacted by the satanic kingdom and filled the land of Panama with murder by killing all those he thought opposed him. The repeated sound of helicopters in the middle of the night meant that more remains of tortured bodies were being dumped somewhere in the jungles. He seemed invincible—until Christian leaders organized to pray. They prayed once a month by radio, traveling throughout the country on buses. Those who had to stay home prayed in agreement with the radio broadcasts. Finally, General Noriega was deposed and sent to an American prison. According to evangelist Luis Palau, Manuel Noriega has since given his life to Jesus Christ.[9]

Our modern-day assignment is the salvation of people and nations. Jesus commissioned us, "Go into all the world and preach the gospel to all creation" (Mark 16:15). Our assignment is birthed in the place of prayer, but we cannot pray effectively until we understand and carry our Father's heart to those He has created.

## Praying for God's Will

So, how do we pray? Remember that Jesus instructed us to pray for God's will to be done on earth as it is in heaven (see Matthew 6:10). Our prayers matter, and God's will does not happen unless we pray. For this reason, we need to use wisdom and think about what we pray before we pray it. As long as we are aligned with God's written Word and His voice, we will release the right things into our world through our prayers and prophetic intercession. If we are not aligned, though, we can "loose" the wrong things (see Matthew 16:19). We are more powerful in prayer than we think.

I know this from personal experience. In an earlier chapter, I mentioned that my husband, Ron, initiated a large remodeling project at our church in 2003 to update our building, as our facility had received little attention since the 1950s. The building had dim lighting; gold-colored, theater-style chairs that smelled; old, musty green carpet; a huge pipe-organ system; metallic gold wallpaper on the sanctuary's largest wall; and other memorabilia from that long-gone era. Also worth mentioning were the cracked exterior paint, the slippery cement lobby floor, the stairwells that led nowhere and the missing foundations on parts of the building. It all had to go!

As a church, we managed to complete our renovation, making the church into a more functional, high-tech and visually pleasing facility, and many families made deep sacrifices to bring this about.

Our biggest issue during the remodel was our city's building department. They approved our construction plans and then reneged on their approval after we began construction. Our sanctuary had been gutted, and now they wanted more safety features included—to the tune of several hundred thousand dollars. If we did not comply with these requirements, they threatened to inspect our extensive building for even more code violations. It was pure extortion and put us in a terrible financial bind.

By the grace of God, we got through it. But I will tell you that as a new prayer community, we prayed a simple prayer over that situation without realizing the extensive ramifications that prayer would have.

All we asked the Lord to do was "change" the building department. I admit we were angry. I admit we wanted justice. I was not in a place of forgiveness by any means, and we kept that prayer for change before the Lord for well over a year after construction had ended.

One day, we heard the news: The entire staff of the building department, including tenured members, had been laid off. That seemed impossible at the time, but it really happened. Unfortunately, this included one of our boardmembers in good standing, who happened to be a building inspector for the city. He had nothing to do with our situation, but I believe he got caught in the crosshairs of our intercession. I did not anticipate the power of our petition and watched our boardmember walk through a difficult job loss as the city government emptied its building department.

I learned a very valuable lesson during that season: We need to think about what we pray before we pray it. We prayed a prayer out of our own hearts without bothering to seek the Lord's heart first, and then our prayer came to pass.

I heard someone pray one time, "Lord, if this certain person keeps drinking, just make him sick!" I normally would not think too much about that kind of thing, except now my experience with the building department had taught me better. What does *sick* look like? If that person takes a drink, do they get cancer or something? Do they throw up? Get ulcers?

I know this seems out there, but you have much power in prayer. I once had a relative pray for her husband to change some behavior. She asked God to "make him sick if He had to." The husband ended up with a degenerative disease and never got healed. God does not use sickness to teach people lessons, which means this person's prayer did not come from heaven. It is a spiritual violation that strikes a bargain with the demonic kingdom to try to manipulate someone's behavior.

Notice what happened when Jesus' disciples experienced rejection by a certain Samaritan village and reported it to Jesus. They asked if they should command fire to come and consume the village, as Elijah did (see Luke 9:51–54 NKJV). I am amazed at their level of faith—they believed they could command fire—but instead of praise, they got a swift rebuke. Jesus said to them, "You do not know what manner of spirit you are of. For the Son of Man did not come to destroy men's lives but to save them" (Luke 9:55–56 NKJV). Notice that Jesus did not say their command could not happen. What He addressed, however, was their hearts, which were in the wrong place.

Have you ever felt as the disciples did after being rejected by someone? Did you suggest to God that they should be punished for what they did to you? These are normal feelings, and we have all experienced them. We struggle to balance our feelings with the redemptive heart of Christ when we are mad, disgusted, appalled or experience injustice. Regardless, we are exhorted to pray and intercede "for all people" (1 Timothy 2:1). Praying for all people is not praying just for the people you like. It is praying for the people you do not like, too, believing they will turn from darkness to light and live victoriously for Jesus Christ.

I will share with you another story of what can go wrong here. I sat in a conference one day next to a middle-aged woman who began to share her story with me. She had been a children's pastor at a church in the Midwest and felt she had discerned her pastor's wife operating in a Jezebel spirit. This is a very involved teaching, but in short, a Jezebel spirit can be characterized by manipulation, control, sexual sin and a counterfeit prophetic gifting. This children's pastor began to pray and ask others to pray with her about the Jezebel spirit controlling her pastor's wife. She believed she had also found proof her pastor's wife had this evil spirit, and she gave her evidence to the church board and a denominational oversight committee. Sadly, the board and the denominational committee agreed and removed the pastor and the pastor's wife from their pulpit.

My mouth fell open as the woman described this. I looked at her and said, "In my church, we don't call anyone a Jezebel, even if they are one."

That got her attention.

Next I said, "Most people we call a Jezebel are just women in process."

I knew I had angered her. I could tell she was not receptive to authority in her life. What I believe really happened was she had become offended at her pastor and his wife. Instead of quitting her position, she chose to use prayer and accusation to remove them from their pulpit. Unfortunately, the board and oversight committee thought and acted just as foolishly. This is not the heart of Christ. It was actually rebellion, even though she felt justified in what she did.

Hearts that are aligned with Jesus and His unfailing love for mankind will not condemn or overthrow. They pray for God's Kingdom and God's will to come into the lives of evil presidents, despots, and greedy businesspeople. They pray through genuine concerns and conflicts in a way that loves and redeems. They do not gather together in prayer to destroy people or nations. They do the opposite, in fact, and command resurrection life to flow into dead places. If you can pray redemptively for those who have angered and offended you, then you know you have the right heart in the matter and that you have maintained your alignment with the Holy Spirit.

Jesus further taught the disciples about prayer through a parable about a widow and an unjust judge (see Luke 18:1–8). In the parable, the widow insists that she get justice from her adversary and pesters the unjust judge day and night about it.

The judge gives in to her demands, not because he cares but because he wants her to stop bothering him.

Through this parable, Jesus is teaching us to pray and not ever give up. He also finishes His story with a question: "When the Son of Man comes, will he find faith on the earth?" (verse 8). That is because faith looks like extreme persistence and becomes a prayer that does not give up.

Our assignment is to pray relentlessly for nations, but Satan will try to convince us to give up praying. How does he do that? He provokes us to be offended at people and nations—because offended people stop praying. He persuades us to believe bad things happening on the earth must be a sign of the times, meaning a sign of Christ's return to earth, and that therefore we should just accept it. If we think that way, we will fail to challenge patterns of destruction in prayer. Satan also tries to convince us God is judging people and nations for their evil, that somehow they have it coming to them, in order to restrain us from praying. There is a day set aside for judgment (see Acts 17:31), but today is not that day. All of these ideas and more are thrown at us intercessors to distract us from our assignment, which is the redemption of nations and the salvation of mankind.

## Praying in Agreement

The Body of Christ needs to be in agreement concerning its assignment. One side of the church prays and shouts a message of extreme grace. The other side prays and shouts the message of God's fiery judgment. Division has created sounds of confusion along the threshing floors of prayer, leaving us spiritually impotent in the bigger, weightier matters. But Jesus taught us to agree together in prayer for the redemption of nations because the sound of agreement is irresistible to our heavenly Father.

When a church prays together, it means they have decided to unite their voices over the same thing before our heavenly Father. This kind of prayer is called the *prayer of agreement*, and our heavenly Father promises to answer this kind of prayer: "Again, truly I tell you that if two of you on earth agree about anything they ask for, it will be done for them by my Father in heaven" (Matthew 18:19). The word *agree* in this verse is the Greek word *symphōneō*. This Greek word is where we get the word *symphony*, and it means "to sound together, to be in unison and to be in accord." The church praying together becomes a pleasant and powerful sound, such as the sound of a well-orchestrated symphony. It is attractive to the ears of our heavenly Father and cultivates a favorable response.

In the beginning of mankind's history, people shared one language and could unite very quickly as a result. We see in Genesis that the people began to build a tower that reached to the heavens (see Genesis 11:4). The Jewish historian Josephus added to this story, saying that Nimrod, the great-grandson of Noah, was angry with God about the Flood. Nimrod convinced the people to turn against God and build a tower too high for waters to reach, and he did this out of spite for the God who had flooded the earth.[10]

Genesis further describes how the Lord came down from heaven to see the tower and what the people were doing. He said, "If as one people speaking the same language they have begun to do this, then nothing they plan to do will be impossible for them. Come, let us go down and confuse their language so they will not understand each other" (verses 6–7). This event took place at the Tower of Babel, where the Lord confounded the people's language. Once their sound was confused, they could no longer unite in their purpose.

In principle, this passage shows us the immense power of a united sound. A united sound means that nothing is impossible. God is a restorer of all things, but He will restore things to a more perfect order. When the believers were praying in the Upper Room and waiting for "the Promise of [the] Father" (Luke 24:49 NKJV), they received the baptism of the Holy Spirit and the gift of supernatural tongues (see Acts 2:4). From there, other believers also received the gift of supernatural tongues as the Holy Spirit fell upon them (see Acts 10:46; 19:6). The gift of tongues is also referred to as a *prayer language*. When we pray in our prayer language, the Holy Spirit intercedes through us in the things that are past our understanding (see Romans 8:26).

The gift of supernatural tongues is in contrast with what God did to the people at the Tower of Babel. A unifying language has been restored to the people of God by the power of the Holy Spirit. This language crosses all natural language barriers and can bring people together in prayer, even if they do not speak the same natural language. I have prayed in my prayer language with people of many different countries and native languages. The gift of tongues allows us to cross our language barriers and unite in prayer with one beautiful sound:

> How wonderful and pleasant it is when brothers live together in harmony! For harmony is as precious as the anointing oil that was poured over Aaron's head, that ran down his beard and onto the border of his robe. Harmony is as refreshing as the dew from Mount Hermon that falls on the mountains of Zion. And there the LORD has pronounced his blessing, even life everlasting.
>
> Psalm 133:1–3 NLT

We receive distinct blessings when we come together in unity before God. The first blessing is the release of the anointing oil.

The oil is a symbol of the Holy Spirit. He pours Himself out on us in power as we unify in prayer (see Acts 2:1–4). Being in unity also refreshes us. Contrast this with the feeling of being drained when you are in discord with other people. The Lord pronounces His distinct blessing on the place where the people have united in prayer. That blessing is a blessing of life. Things will live again.

## Praying in Your Church

A church that prays together offers an outstanding display of unity that attracts the blessings of heaven. Many churches desire to have a vibrant prayer community but do not know how to build one or sustain one. Prayer is taught, but it is mostly caught. There are both practical and spiritual applications to consider.

When it comes to creating a vibrant prayer culture at our places of worship, recognize that prayer is built like a muscle. We start small and then build over time. It is also a relational ministry and therefore needs to emphasize a community component. People come to a prayer service not only to pray and encounter God, but also to find friendship with other intercessors.

There are a variety of things to consider when building a prayer community, but here are the ones I think are the most important:

### 1. Set a Prayer Time

The Scriptures speak of a set time for prayer: "One day Peter and John were going up to the temple *at the time of prayer*—at three in the afternoon" (Acts 3:1, emphasis added). Accordingly, set a regular time to gather for prayer, and commit to it. Our first prayer service was on a Saturday night for

164

one hour. We still have that prayer service, but we also have many other prayer times now offered throughout the week and on weekends.

## 2. Choose a Prayer Location

I am one of those people who can pray anywhere and at any time. I do not need music or props to experience prayer. When I worked in the corporate world, I would retreat to a bathroom stall for prayer. I think my co-workers thought I had a digestive problem! I didn't. I was just praying.

I realize, however, that most people are not like me and need a special getaway space for prayer. Again, Peter and John went to the Temple for prayer. The Temple was a meaningful space that was ready to receive prayers. You can designate a room in your church, meet at a person's home or find other meaningful locations in your city to meet for prayer.

## 3. Choose a Prayer Leader

Our first prayer leader could not sustain a week-to-week commitment, so I became the prayer leader for our weekly Saturday prayer service. Leading a community in consistent prayer requires inner strength, commitment and stamina. Prayer leaders need to have humble hearts, a strong prayer life, a sound biblical foundation, good relationship skills and the ability to gather others to prayer. I also insist our prayer leaders carry a heartbeat for the local church and demonstrate loyalty toward those in church leadership.

I do not believe all prayer gatherings need to be directly connected to one church or another, but whoever leads them needs to be mindful to build in prayer what Jesus is building. He is building His Church to shine in every community.

## 4. Plan Your Prayer Service

Prayer services need to be life-giving and experiential, which requires good planning and ideas to keep attendees focused and interested. Before the prayer gathering, prepare some prayer points and Scriptures, and perhaps also prepare some light teaching or exhortation. The prayer leader communicates specific prayer directives and then facilitates the prayer service in various ways with the people in attendance. We also instruct our prayer leaders to pray in alignment with the mission of our church, as established by my husband and me.

## 5. Deal with Problem People

Very rarely do I come across a problem person in our prayer sessions, but it does happen. This might be a person who uses the prayer time to preach or who dominates the room with unusually long and loud praying. Other problem people do not follow the prayer leader's directives and attempt to redirect the prayer time to their own interests. This is usually done in ignorance but needs to be confronted. You should never let one person ruin the prayer time for others.

## Praying as You Go

I believe God has been preparing you, through this book, for greater intercession. In some ways, God has allowed me to be a forerunner in prayer so I could give you road-tested keys and help you navigate some trickier terrain.

As you step into your unique journey of prayer, your awareness of God's voice will deepen in meaningful ways. Remember that prayer is first a dialogue between you and God, full of intimate, precious moments that make praying a "want to" rather than a "have to." At the same time, the Holy Spirit will beckon you into strategic intercession for others. You will watch history unfold as your words before the Father transform into winds of change for the very thing you brought before Him. Prayer is no little matter. It is power, and praying people are powerful people. You will become one who thwarts demonic plans within your *metron* as you prepare the way for hell's prisoners to be released to receive salvation. The Holy Spirit delights in you and cherishes your partnership in prayer.

As you have read and digested the principles in this book, have you noticed a greater sensitivity to the Spirit and the spiritual realm growing within you? An intercessor encounters a wide variety of spiritual happenings, as the spiritual realm is set in motion by our prophetic intercession. Angels, demons, the voice of God, intercessory dreams, visions and prophetic encounters are normal in the life of an intercessor. As problems arise, we are quick to discern the root causes of them so we can pray effectively. To the intercessor, no problem is impossible. It just needs the right spiritual key, something you will search out in the Word and in prayer until you find it and apply it effectively.

Whenever God intends to do something on the earth, an intercessor is on the scene long before anything happens. These intercessors are friends of God, and God shares His secrets with His friends. You are one such friend. He will tell you what He plans to do and bring you in to be a part of it.

Do not be surprised when the Lord sends you on secret missions to secret locations to pray, to perform prophetic acts and to make scriptural declarations. As His ambassador, do not be shocked when He opens doors for you to pray for and speak to men and women of influence in the nations. This is the life of the intercessor. Where He sends you, you will go. You are part of an elite force in His private army of saints. It is humbling to be a part of something so great.

Are you ready to experience the adventures of prayer? There is always more! The journey of prayer never stops unfolding. Someday we will meet each other and see the impact our lives have made. I believe we will be awestruck at how many people and nations were preserved, rescued and saved because we lived to intercede.

## Kingdom Prayer Principles

1. Prayer is the first ministry of the modern-day Church. The reach of our prayers is the nations.

2. We govern our whole world with prayer. Prayer is the most powerful exercise of godly authority on the earth.

3. A praying Church overturns demonic plans, puts angels on assignment, cleanses atmospheres and creates conditions for the visible invasion of the Word of God into the nations.

4. We need to cultivate and embrace a lifestyle of prayer.

5. Christians who do not pray or do not make an effort to pray as a church community forfeit their authority. They do not realize they are the reason many people remain hell-chained in their communities with no other way of deliverance.

6. Everything rises or falls on the prayers of the Church.

7. We need to use wisdom and think about what we pray before we pray it. We are more powerful in prayer than we think.

8. We are to pray redemptively for all people and all nations, not just the people we like. Judgment and offense in our hearts are hindrances to prayer.

## Thoughts for Reflection

1. Prayer is the first priority of the Church. How do you prioritize prayer when life always seems so busy?

2. What does a lifestyle of prayer look like? How do you cultivate that?

3. Do you struggle to pray for people, leaders or nations that are evil? How do you overcome that in your heart?

4. Have you ever prayed for social issues? What social issues drive you to your knees in prayer?

5. Do you have a prayer language? What was your experience of receiving it?

## Appendix A

# The Key Differences Between Christians and Latter-Day Saints (Mormons)

As I mentioned in the first chapter of this book, I grew up in the Latter-Day Saints (LDS) church. I was an active member, immersed in Mormon beliefs and a participant in some of their temple rituals.

The temple rituals varied but usually involved religious acts on behalf of someone who had died. For example, I would be baptized in water on behalf of another person who had died, in order to fulfill their eternal requirement for baptism. None of the rituals were perverse or scary but were done to secure aspects of the afterlife for the ones who had passed on.

As a Mormon, I learned about the importance of family, of tithing and of being physically healthy. I was taught good character and modesty as a woman. I was also taught a framework for the existence of modern-day prophets, heavenly revelations, angelic visitations, the Holy Ghost and the idea that the gifts of the Holy Ghost were to be embraced. (I prefer to say Holy Spirit, but an LDS member will take care to say Holy Ghost.)

LDS followers use terminology that sounds similar to the terminology Christians use. Keep in mind that these things may sound the same but have different meanings underneath. For example, Mormons believe Jesus Christ is their Lord and Savior and died for their sins so they can have eternity in heaven. This is the same statement of faith as Christians, except the Jesus embraced by the LDS church and the Jesus of the Christian faith are not the same Jesus.

Mormons believe we preexisted in heaven. They also believe in eternal families, past and future. Eternal families are marital unions in heaven that produce children. In the LDS belief structure, God the Father had a beginning, and so did Jesus Christ. Jesus was titled the firstborn Son because He was born first. They believe the rest of us were born in like manner as Jesus.

They also believe Lucifer was a rebellious brother in our spirit family, rather than a rebellious archangel. Instead of taking a third of the angels with him in his rebellion, LDS members believe Lucifer took one-third of God's spirit children into his allegiance. These rebellious brothers and sisters who existed in heaven before mankind appeared on the earth now manifest as evil people on earth and are forever condemned.

Christians do not believe we preexisted in heaven. Instead, they believe we were perfectly preknown and planned for in the heart of God, as He is all-knowing and knows our beginning from our end. King David wrote, "All the days ordained for me were written in your book before one of them came to be" (Psalm 139:16).

We also do not accept that Lucifer, also known as Satan, is a spiritual brother. Rather, Satan is a fallen angel that ranked in authority alongside the archangels Michael and Gabriel. He had charge of one-third of the angelic host, who rebelled with him and are now manifest as demons on the earth.

Christians also shun the idea of marriage, sexual union and childbearing in a heavenly context. For human beings, there is no eternal plan for marriage or childbearing in heaven, based on the words of Jesus in Mark 12:25: "When the dead rise, they will neither marry nor be given in marriage; they will be like the angels in heaven."

The LDS church refers to four scriptural texts: the Bible, the Book of Mormon, the Doctrine and Covenants, and the Pearl of Great Price. The founder of the LDS church, Joseph Smith, claims to have received the Book of Mormon after an angel named Moroni visited him and revealed to him the book's location. Smith claims to have found a set of inscribed gold plates buried at the Hill Cumorah in New York. These inscriptions were then interpreted through supernatural means, and the result was the Book of Mormon. I read the Book of Mormon a handful of times while growing up. It is a proposed historical narrative between Jesus and early Native Americans.

The Doctrine and Covenants is a book that contains their church standards and beliefs. It is comparable to the book of Proverbs. The Pearl of Great Price offers an additional narrative, similar to the Book of Mormon, and includes a Book of Moses.

When it comes to an LDS prophet, his words and decrees can supersede anything written in their holy texts and carries the most weight. The leader of the LDS church is always given the title of prophet and is chosen out of their Quorum of the Twelve Apostles. This explains how stances held by the LDS church over the years have shifted, as doctrine is not anchored in their written texts.

Conversely, Christians hold to one scriptural text: the Bible. Many Christians believe in modern-day apostles and prophets, as described in Ephesians 4:11–12, but the word of the prophet must submit to the Bible, not the other way around. Prophets cannot create theology that is not already communicated in Scripture.

In Christendom, prophets often predict the future with accuracy and operate in powerful signs and wonders. At the same time, they do not have absolute authority over the Church. They are part of a governing structure chosen by Jesus, which includes apostles, evangelists, pastors and teachers. Together, these persons lead the Church on earth with the goal of equipping the saints for ministry and bringing them to maturity.

An interesting paradox exists between LDS and Christian communities when it comes to beliefs about the supernatural. I have found the LDS framework to be more biblical than that held by many Christian denominations, especially the cessationist denominations, such as the Southern Baptist, Church of Christ, Evangelical Free and Reformed churches. For example, LDS members believe in apostles and prophets, the gifts of the Spirit as listed in 1 Corinthians 12:8–10, the activity of angels, the active voice of God through the prophets and personally, and the receiving of spiritual revelations. Although their application is misplaced, a biblical framework somehow emerged through Joseph Smith.

The last key difference between Christians and Mormons is the LDS belief in personal deification. They are actively striving to progress in this life so they can become a god in the next. I never understood this to be a competitive statement against the Creator, but rather a by-product of having become like Christ in the way they believe Him to be. Remember that Mormons believe Jesus had a beginning and progressed to His place of deity. They are attempting to do the same. This drives many Mormons to be successful and promotes a sense of excellence within their ranks.

Christians, on the other hand, believe they are made in the image of God, are full of the Holy Spirit and carry a heavenly mandate on earth. Although we would hardly refer to ourselves as gods, we do embrace our spiritual titles—that of kings and priests on earth—having been given all authority in Jesus' name. Love and compassion for mankind drives us into successful action more than a fearful striving for rank and title in heaven. In an eternal context, Christians are content to forever worship their God, dwell in heavenly mansions, enjoy fellowship with the Son and anticipate the new Jerusalem. It is an eternal rest we seek, not deification, since we will all be changed instantly at the last trumpet and be given glorious bodies at the resurrection of the dead (see 1 Corinthians 15:52).

# How to Deliver a Person from Demons

When I was a new Christian, I attended a large Pentecostal church for a short while, just before I met my husband, Ron. It was a great church, and I enjoyed being with people my age who were excited about God.

One Sunday, I met a few older women who said they had a special prayer meeting happening in another part of the building. They invited me to come, so I went.

Unfortunately, they had taken it upon themselves to start a deliverance session with me without my permission. When I say they started a deliverance session, what I mean is they tried to cast a variety of spirits out of me—except that I never manifested any such spirits and their methods felt really spooky.

I liked the church and so I kept attending, but I avoided those women from that point on. Every so often, they would find me in the service and try to convince me to get more prayer from them. No, thank you! It is funny to me now, but I did learn from that experience and a few others like it what to do and what *not* to do when it comes to deliverance ministry.

What is deliverance ministry? Jesus said that when we preach the Gospel, we can expect to encounter the following: "And these signs will accompany those who believe: In my name they will drive out demons" (Mark 16:17). This means that when we are sharing the Gospel, we will encounter people controlled by demons, and these spirits will need to be cast out.

How do we know when someone has a demon? And if they do, how do we cast them out? In this section, I will give you some basics to help you minister effectively when you encounter a person possessed by spirits. These are general guidelines. For more detailed instructions, I recommend *Free in Christ* by Pablo Bottari and *I Give You Authority* by Charles H. Kraft.

## 1. Care for people, not their demons.

Jesus sent the 72 disciples, two by two, into all the places He was intending to go and minister. They came back, reporting with joy, "Lord, even the demons submit to us in your name" (Luke 10:17). Jesus responded by acknowledging their God-given authority over such spirits but clarified what was most important: "Do not rejoice that the spirits submit to you, but rejoice that your names are written in heaven" (verse 20). In other words, casting out demons is important, but the fate of each person is more important.

When you encounter a situation that requires you to deliver someone from spirits, take care to preserve their dignity. Do not humiliate them or abuse them in the process, as this could drive a wedge between them and God and His Church. For example:

> Do not yell or scream at the demons inside people. Spirits respond to authority, not volume.

Do not expose them in front of a crowd, if you can help it. Take them somewhere private.

Take care to alleviate any fears they might have. (For instance, I do not tell people they are possessed. I explain they are exhibiting spiritual problems, and then I ask them if they want to be free.)

Show them love and care through the process.

## 2. Make sure they have manifested.

Just as physical diseases reveal themselves through a series of symptoms, so do people afflicted with demonic spirits reveal symptoms. Some symptoms, also known as manifestations, are obvious, and others are not so obvious and require investigation.

For example, we have had people respond in church services to the presence of the Holy Spirit with what sounds like a scream, followed by a collapse on the floor. Would you believe this is not necessarily a demonic manifestation? When this happens, I often ask the person, who is usually shaking on the floor, "What's happening? Is this God or something else?" They can always tell me. Sometimes it is God, and others times it is demonic. Depending on their answer, we either leave them alone to enjoy His presence or we begin to address the spirit afflicting them.

Other symptoms we have determined to be demonic manifestations include:

Sudden onset of jerky, almost violent movements

Catatonic state

Growling or hissing

Sudden outburst of expletives

Sudden physical ailments (but investigate—sudden nausea or headaches could be demonic manifestations or an alert from the Holy Spirit that someone nearby needs healing)
Distorted face or contorted body
Hostile look

This is a basic list, and it can get more complex, depending on the bondage and how rooted it is. Either way, when you see these behaviors come upon a person, it is time to take redemptive action.

### 3. Make sure they want to be free.

I recall a time more than a decade ago when a kind, middle-aged gentleman began coming to our weekly prayer services and attending our church on Sundays. During one of the prayer services, he was seated behind me, worshiping in song, and began to sing in his prayer language. The only thing is, his prayer language did not sound right.

I have noticed over the years that when a person around me has a demonic spirit that is beginning to manifest, I become agitated and annoyed. My mind usually does not know what is happening, but the Holy Spirit in me is reacting to the demon nearby.

As this man continued to sing with strange sounds, I turned around and said, without thinking, "Be quiet!"

When I did that, he cussed me out and began running around the sanctuary, shouting repeatedly, "You can't cast me out!"

A few of us tried to get him to be still. We did not physically touch him, but we commanded the spirit to be bound and then asked him to let us help him. He would not allow us to help. Instead, he ran out of the building and into the parking lot. When he came back inside, we pleaded again for him to let us help.

All we received in return was more glaring and cussing before he ran out the door for the last time. We never saw him again.

We have experienced many persons exhibiting much stronger demonic manifestations than this man, but those other people received our help and, in turn, their deliverance. What made the difference? Almost always, the difference was in their will. Not everyone is ready to face what he or she needs to face in order to be delivered. Or they simply do not want to be free. One young man explained why he would not receive ministry, even though he had manifested in front of us. He said, "I like the power coming from that spirit, and I don't want to give it up."

You see, not everyone wants to be free. When they do not want freedom, you cannot force it to happen. But when they are ready, they will not run away. They may present a strong demonic manifestation, but they will submit themselves to the process of deliverance, because inside they really want to be free.

## 4. Put them in control of their deliverance.

Our first goal when a person has manifested demonically is to bind the spirit and bring the person to consciousness so we can lead them to deliver themselves, if possible. The way we bind the demonic spirit is by using our words and making a command with authority (see Matthew 18:18; Mark 11:23). Here are a couple of suggestions:

"I stop all demonic manifestations, in Jesus' name."
"Submit yourself, in Jesus' name."

Next, we tell the person to take control of their body and mind, which puts them back in control. Then we discuss with them what needs to happen next.

If the person is not a Christian, we invite them to receive Jesus as their Lord and Savior, as they will not be able to maintain their deliverance without having done this. I have found that some people want the spirit to be gone but do not want to submit to Christ, and some do not want to stop the behavior that invited demonization in the first place. As much as it pains me, I cannot proceed with deliverance in these instances, because it opens them up to even worse demonization. Jesus described to us what happens when an unclean spirit leaves a man. He said it goes and finds seven more spirits worse than itself, and they enter and possess the person, making "the last state of that man . . . worse than the first" (Luke 11:26 NKJV). When a person receives Christ, they also receive an initial infilling of the Holy Spirit, which is all they need to prevent a disastrous repossession.

Now, the person has manifested because the demonic spirit has been given access somehow. This is where you need to ask a few questions and listen to the Holy Spirit to find out why that demon is there. Typically, the point of access is in one of four main areas: fear, hatred, the occult or sexual sin. In a pastoral manner, we begin to ask the following questions:

What or whom do you fear?

Whom do you hate?

Have you participated in any occult activities, or has your family?

Do you have sexual sin in your present or past, or has anyone sinned against you sexually?

I do not ask these questions all at once, but rather one at a time, and I listen to what they say while sensing what the Holy Spirit is saying.

After each admission, we coach the person to ask Jesus to forgive them for the specific trespass, or we coach them to forgive those who trespassed against them. Then we have them renounce—out loud—any spirit that may have come in as a result. When the spirit leaves, some type of release will be felt or seen. This could be a cough, a sigh, a physical shake or something like it. Pay attention to those signals. This means the spirit has left them.

### 5. Have them receive the baptism of the Holy Spirit.

This is the best part! Jesus said, "You shall receive power when the Holy Spirit has come upon you" (Acts 1:8 NKJV). Once the person has renounced demonic spirits, they need to be baptized in the Holy Spirit or receive fresh refilling (see Ephesians 5:18).

Lay your hands on them and ask Jesus to baptize them or fill them again with the Holy Spirit. You will often feel or see His power come upon them, and they will physically manifest, but in a different way now. If they do not have a prayer language, encourage them to speak the Spirit's language as they feel it bubble up from inside. Celebrate any manifestation of the Spirit they may encounter. This type of ending is encouraging to the participant, as it connects them to God and they receive His embrace in a meaningful way.

### 6. Provide good follow-up care.

Make sure to follow up with the person receiving deliverance in a way that is caring and supportive. They will need to process and talk through any spiritual happenings that show up after they are delivered. For example, they may experience nightmares or receive a demonic visitation, or someone from their past may reemerge. They will need encouragement and fellowship when this happens, as well as reminders of how to continue in their newfound freedom.

Again, these are just the basics of how to minister to a person who is demonized. You may encounter some situations or people who do not respond to these simple steps, requiring you to do more to see them all the way into freedom. Look at those situations as opportunities to learn something new about Jesus and the spiritual realm—and trust the Holy Spirit to give you the right keys to unlock prison doors.

# Notes

### Chapter 1: My Lifeline for Victory

1. The LDS church appears similar to Christianity on the surface but is very different in theology underneath. You can read about those differences in appendix A.

2. According to its denominational website, the United Pentecostal Church emerged out of the Pentecostal movement that began with a Bible school in Topeka, Kansas, in 1901 and with the Azusa Street Revival in Los Angeles, California, in 1906. It traces its organizational roots to 1916, when a large group of Pentecostal ministers began to unite around the teaching of the oneness of God and water baptism in the name of Jesus Christ.

### Chapter 2: The Basics of Prayer

1. E. M. Bounds, *The Weapon of Prayer* (Radford, Va.: Wilder Books, 2008), 8.

2. Watchman Nee, *The Prayer Ministry of the Church* (Anaheim, Calif.: Living Stream Ministry, 1993), 22.

### Chapter 3: Who's in Charge?

1. Cindy Jacobs, "Cindy Jacobs: How Do We Biblically Intercede to Overcome the Strongman?" The Elijah List, August 23, 2013, http://www.elijahlist.com /words/display_word.html?ID=12480 (accessed October 30, 2015).

### Chapter 5: Are Territorial Spirits Real?

1. Chapter 12 of the book of Revelation is a common reference for the existence of demons. It describes in prophetic language how Satan was expelled from heaven to the earth, taking one-third of the angels with him.

2. See *Matthew Poole's Commentary* on Daniel 10:2, as quoted at Bible Hub, http://biblehub.com/commentaries/poole/daniel/10.htm.

3. Tom White, *The Believer's Guide to Spiritual Warfare* (Ventura, Calif.: Regal, 2011), 55.

4. John Paul Jackson, *Needless Casualties of War* (Fort Worth, Tex.: Streams Publications, 1999), 62.

### Chapter 6: God's Mighty Invisible Army

1. The Holy Spirit's gift of discernment of spirits is mentioned in 1 Corinthians 12:10. It is a supernatural ability to distinguish between spirits and their motives—divine, demonic or human.

### Chapter 7: Prophetic Intercession

1. Kenneth Copeland, *The Power of the Tongue* (Tulsa, Okla.: Harrison House, 1980).

2. Mark and Patti Virkler, *Four Keys to Hearing God's Voice* (Shippensburg, Pa.: Destiny Image, 2010), 24–25.

3. Barbara Wentroble, *Prophetic Intercession* (Ventura, Calif.: Regal, 2003), 67.

### Chapter 8: Fasting Is a Game Changer

1. Mike Bickle, "The Unlikely Ambassador," *Loving God* (blog), *Charisma*, http://www.charismamag.com/spirit/devotionals/loving-god?view=article&id =2365:the-unlikely-ambassador&catid=146.

2. Elmer Towns, *The Beginner's Guide to Fasting* (Ventura, Calif.: Regal, 2001), 123–124.

### Chapter 9: How to Pray Intelligently

1. The story is told in Helen Alma Hohenthal, *Streams in a Thirsty Land: A History of the Turlock Region* (Turlock, Calif.: City of Turlock, 1972).

2. Dutch Sheets, *Watchman Prayer: How to Stand Guard and Protect Your Family, Home and Community* (Ventura, Calif.: Regal, 2000), 33.

### Chapter 10: We Are a House of Prayer

1. Kim Catherine Marie Kollins, as quoted in Pete Greig and Dave Roberts, *Red Moon Rising: How 24-7 Prayer Is Awakening a Generation* (Lake Mary, Fla.: Relevant Books, 2003), 137.

2. Daniel Okrent, *Last Call: The Rise and Fall of Prohibition* (New York: Scribner, 2010), 7.

3. Ibid., 9.

4. Abraham Lincoln, "Temperance Address," February 22, 1842, Teaching AmericanHistory.org, http://teachingamericanhistory.org/library/document /temperance-address/.

5. See http://ichilly.com/bio.

6. Tom Phillips, "China On Course to Become 'World's Most Christian Nation' within 15 Years," *The Telegraph*, April 19, 2014, http://www.telegraph.co.uk/news/worldnews/asia/china/10776023/China-on-course-to-become-worlds-most-Christian-nation-within-15-years.html.

7. George Otis Jr., *Transformations* (1999; The Sentinel Group, Lynnwood, Wash.), video.

8. Sunday Adelaja, *Church Shift: Revolutionizing Your Faith, Church and Life for the 21st Century* (Lake Mary, Fla.: Charisma House, 2008), 117; and Bickle, "The Unlikely Ambassador."

9. Cindy Jacobs, "Overcome the Strongman and Tremendous Revival Breaks Forth," *The Elijah List*, August 23, 2013, http://www.elijahlist.com/words/display_word.html?ID=12480; and Ravi Zacharias, "Noriega's New Commander," *Men of Integrity* (blog), *Christianity Today*, March 4, 2001, http://www.christianitytoday.com/moi/2001/002/march/noriegas-new-commander.html.

10. Flavius Josephus, *Antiquities of the Jews,* book 1, chapter 4, as quoted at http://penelope.uchicago.edu/josephus/ant-1.html.

Jennifer Eivaz is a vibrant minister and international conference speaker who carries the wisdom and fire of the Holy Spirit. She serves as an executive pastor with Harvest Christian Center in Turlock, California, and is focused on raising up a passionate and effective prayer community that is tempered with love and hears the voice of God accurately.

Jennifer loves the presence of God and is a prophetic voice to many. Her teaching style is authentic and aimed at the heart, having been built on her personal testimony of God's incredible goodness and miraculous display in her life and in the life of her church.

Jennifer is a graduate of Oral Roberts University in Tulsa, Oklahoma. She is married to Harvest Christian Center's senior pastor, Ron Eivaz, and they have two wonderful children.

## Connect with Jennifer

Facebook: www.facebook.com/jennifereivaz/
Twitter: @prayingprophet
Instagram: @prayingprophet
Blog: www.jennifereivazblog.com
YouTube: www.youtube.com/user/JenEivaz
Periscope: Jennifer Eivaz
Catch the Jennifer Eivaz podcast on iTunes

"There is no other writer out there who I have seen do as good a job as Jennifer Eivaz when it comes to writing and teaching on intercession. I don't know how she does it, frankly, but Jennifer is able to pack into a paragraph or two an afternoon's worth of teaching and study. What she explains is easy to grasp yet profound when put into application. Get *The Intercessors Handbook*, one for you and two for friends!"

Steve Shultz, founder, The Elijah List

"*The Intercessors Handbook* is both a journey and a classroom. It carries the depth of uncovering deep layers of a biblical foundation in prayer/intercession while putting flesh on it through Jen's personal history. Over and over, I found myself personally challenged and inspired to take my personal intercession deeper. Tools are given to elevate both your knowledge and faith in this needed area. Jen also does a masterful job in breaking down the topic in such a way that those who don't consider themselves gifted in this area can track and grow in this ministry. This is a must-read for all who want to contend for all that God wants to release, both individually and corporately."

Sean Smith, director, Sean Smith Ministries /
Pointblank International

"The topic of prayer is one that is often avoided not because people don't have a heart to pray, but because they feel uncertain of how to pray or where to start. Yet prayer is a foundational aspect of our lives as followers of Jesus. Jennifer Eivaz has written a challenging and practical book that is much needed for the church. Rather than written from a place of theory, *The Intercessors Handbook* is written from biblical foundations and principles that have been lived out, not only by Jennifer but by the community she leads. As someone who has lived a life of prayer, she shows us a map of how to pray and ignites within us a passion to embrace the journey of prayer that is the privilege and responsibility of every believer."

Banning Liebscher, founder and pastor, Jesus Culture

"The history of our ministry is written in our prayer life. We must brush away the cobwebs that have obscured true intercession if we want to win this generation. Here is your handbook."

Mario Murillo, president, Mario Murillo Ministries

"Jennifer is forceful and to-the-point in *The Intercessors Handbook*. She helps us realize some critical issues concerning spiritual warfare that many of us have never been taught. The book guides us to a fresh dimension into the domain of spiritual authority and helps us to better recognize that invisible world that co-exists with this natural, physical realm, and how to deal with it successfully. Chapter 10 is especially helpful for pastors who want to establish an effective and dynamic intercessory prayer ministry."

Dr. Dave Williams, bishop, Mount Hope Church
Network; Strategic Global Mission

"Jennifer Eivaz has done a wonderful job of bringing brilliant insight and practical application to the sometimes intimidating subject of intercession. Learning to hear the voice of God is one of the most compelling journeys ever offered us. Unfortunately, we usually turn it into a nearly impossible religious activity. Yet it is God who takes upon Himself the responsibility to be heard. If that weren't enough, God also listens for and loves to respond to our voice. This is the power of intercession—our voice yielded to God's heart helps to create a powerful force that ushers in the manifestation of God's Kingdom on earth. I encourage you to read *The Intercessors Handbook* and be changed. The gift of grace released will enable all who read it to bring about transformational change in our world!"

Bill Johnson, senior leader, Bethel Church, Redding,
California; author, *When Heaven Invades Earth*
and *The Power That Changes the World*

"This easy-to-read book is full of gems that will keep you sane in the midst of conflict, help you think, and stretch your understanding of the supernatural. It opens a door of insight that inspires us to grasp how heaven works with us on earth to strengthen our authority to make Jesus great in the land! Jennifer has a unique style, and her comprehension of the spiritual realms enables her to give clear instruction for many areas of warfare prayer. Anyone who is involved in church planting or establishing prayer teams should read this book. One of the strengths of this book is that it is rooted in the local church and has a heart for the church to flourish. Jennifer's examples and stories are inspiring and encourage you to stand, fight and prevail."

Rachel Hickson, founder and director, Heartcry for
Change; author, *Eat the Word, Speak the Word*

*THE*
# INTERCESSORS
# HANDBOOK